Understanding

J.
s Lea

Also by Trevor Butt

Invitation to Personal Construct Psychology (with Vivien Burr) 1992

Understanding People

TREVOR BUTT

First published 2004 by
PALGRAVE MACMILLAN
Houndmills, Basingstoke, Hampshire RG21 6XS and
175 Fifth Avenue, New York, N.Y. 10010
Companies and representatives throughout the world

PALGRAVE MACMILLAN is the global academic imprint of the Palgrave
Macmillan division of St. Martin's Press, LLC and of Palgrave Macmillan Ltd.
Macmillan® is a registered trademark in the United States, United Kingdom
and other countries. Palgrave is a registered trademark in the European
Union and other countries.

ISBN 1–4039–04650 hardback
ISBN 1–4039–04669 paperback

This book is printed on paper suitable for recycling and made from fully
managed and sustained forest sources.

A catalogue record for this book is available from the British Library.

A catalog record for this book is available from the Library of Congress.

10   9   8   7   6   5   4   3   2   1
13 12 11 10 09 08 07 06 05 04

Typeset in Great Britain by
Aarontype Limited, Easton, Bristol

Printed in China

Contents

Preface

Understanding People seems at first glance a rather pretentious title for a book. When my friends in the clinical world have asked me what the title was to be, a common reaction has been something like 'well, if I give you a couple of names, perhaps you'll let me know what makes them tick'. So first of all, I should say what I mean by understanding. I have spent most of my professional life involved in personal construct theory (PCT) and naturally think in terms of dichotomous constructs. To know what something means you have to see what its contrast is. Understanding versus explaining is a construct that Dilthey (1988) used in the nineteenth century, arguing that the social sciences should not be concerned with causal explanations. Instead they should concentrate on understanding people in the same way that one understands a text. When we read something, we get an appreciation of what it means by moving between part and whole, looking at a word and seeing how it fits into a sentence. So, for example, we only know what 'train' means when we see that it is used as a verb rather than a noun. Similarly, the meaning of a sentence only becomes clear when we can place it in a larger context. When someone says of a partner, 'Yes, I've got him well-trained', we know that the meaning is somewhat ironic. At the same time, the meaning of the whole relies on the parts and a sentence only has meaning by virtue of the words that constitute it. But psychology is the social science most enamoured with the natural sciences and has usually sought meaning by looking for causal explanations at a more molecular level. The psychology of personality has largely been a project engaged in trying to find the causes of individuals' behaviour, either inside them or in the environment.

Now, causal explanations might have a place in psychology, and one could argue that the explanation versus understanding construct is too crude to capture what personality theorists have been up to. So perhaps explanation is a particular type of understanding and not a simple contrast to it. Nonetheless, I maintain that it is a useful distinction, one that draws our attention to what is frequently missing in

This is what I have done in my thesis - Put in Conclusion & intro.

the science of personality – an understanding that does not rely solely on an ability to tell us what kick-starts the person into action. In my view, understanding people requires two things: their account of their reasons and how the world appears to them as well as an appreciation of the social context in which they are embedded. By moving our focus from one to the other and back again, we can begin to make sense of what people do, feel and think. This corresponds roughly to what Ricoeur (1970) describes as a 'hermeneutics of belief' or empathy and a 'hermeneutics of suspicion'. An interpretation based on empathy has to be balanced with one that takes into account things that the person might not, or even cannot, know. The psychologist has to start with how things appear to people, but must not stop there. It may be that unconscious forces or the discursive field within which one moves are not apparent to actors themselves. People might not be in a position to know exactly why they think, feel and act as they do. Interestingly, while personality theorists have been largely looking 'inside' people for answers, a very different approach to the person has been evolving in social psychology. Social constructionism (Burr, 1995) can be thought of as a family of approaches that emphasise the role of social forces, particularly language, in the production of individual action. Kenneth Gergen (2001), the originator of this approach, has made some bold moves towards transcending the agency versus structure issue. This is the debate about whether human action is the product of the individual agent or social forces that determine them (see Walsh, 1998). Determinism might play no part in Gergen's thinking but my contention is that, in the UK at least, variants of social constructionism represent a pendulum swing away from individual agency and towards an overestimation of the forces of social structure. Causal explanations beckon not from within the person, but from ideologies and discourse that move people in ways of which they are not aware.

So how are we to conceptualise the person? My answer to this question is based on a mixture of the pragmatism of both George Kelly and George Mead and the existential phenomenology of Maurice Merleau-Ponty. Interestingly, Berger and Luckmann (1967), on whose work social constructionism has built, drew on both pragmatism and existential phenomenology. Their work conceptualised the individual as a social construction, but nevertheless a centre for agency and choice once constructed. For contemporary social constructionism, it is therefore flawed in that it preserves a mythical sense of personal agency. But I want to return to this conception and elaborate the interpretive, interactionist, agentic constructionism that is inherent and sometimes explicit in pragmatism and existential phenomenology. As you read this last sentence, you might think I've swallowed a psychological dictionary. And this has been my main problem in writing: what do I call the position that I am advocating? I could make up yet another new term or phrase, but I think that both social psychology and personality theory are already overfull with old wine in new bottles. So I have decided to stick to an older vocabulary – that of existential phenomenology. I have chosen this because it seems to me to be an overarching theoretical position that can subsume the pragmatism of Kelly (1955) and Mead (1934), both of whose work considerably extends existentialist thinking. I see myself still as a construct theorist, but my view of PCT is not orthodox or accepted uncritically within the PCT world. I see it as a species of existential phenomenology, albeit one that does not use the somewhat mystifying vocabulary of this approach (see Holland, 1977; Butt, 1998). Pragmatism was an American philosophical movement that developed in parallel with existentialism and phenomenology in Europe. (Interested students should read Menand's (2002) fascinating and compulsively readable history of pragmatism.) In many ways the two approaches complement each other, although their emphases are often different (Rosenthal and Bourgeois, 1991). So in this book, I have chosen to sail under the flag of existential phenomenology, sometimes mentioning pragmatism and interactionism as signposts to help the reader. One cost of this strategy is that I do use that terminology that Keen (1975) says English speakers find odd and even irritating. Phrases like 'being-in-the-world' have been translated directly from German, where the compound nouns have been rendered into somewhat clumsy English equivalents. But 'being-in-the-world' is a concept that I want to promote. The thesis of this book is that understanding people means recognising that we are both all alike and at the same time all different. Psychology has often ignored how we are all beings in the same world, a commonality of situation and culture that enables us to communicate with each other at all. And structural sociology has often forgotten that the way we experience the world is very different, and in this sense we are beings in different worlds. Such concepts are therefore central to this book, as we struggle to make sense of both ourselves and others.

Another problem with calling my position existential phenomenology is that most theorists in this field would dislike my bringing the work of Mead and Kelly under the existential phenomenological umbrella. The closer you get to theories and approaches, the more apparent are the differences between them. But I have chosen to emphasise the similarities between existential phenomenology and pragmatism. This is because, in my view, they share enough common ground that marks them out as different from other approaches to personality. So, they both stress the importance of individual perspectives and first-person accounts in understanding people. Yet both recognise the complex relationship between the person and the social world. In the other personality theories reviewed in subsequent chapters, there is an implicit assumption that the person precedes society. By this I mean that they view the person as a social atom and society as an amalgam of the individuals that make it up. They do not take seriously the proposition that society acts back on the individuals in it and, in an important sense, we are each the product of our society.

It will make most sense to read this work in the order that it is presented. I have tried to write it as a coherent story, taking the reader through from one chapter to the next. If you decide to read it differently, I have cross-referenced wherever possible, so that you can see in which chapters various points are elaborated. To avoid any clumsiness in the use of pronouns, I have used he and she in alternate chapters. In Part I, I briefly review different personality approaches. A theme that emerges is that traditional approaches to personality are rooted in two problematic dualisms: one that separates mind from body and one that separates the individual from society. This leads to an explanatory enterprise that seeks causes of behaviour. I then review social constructionism, arguing that it breaks the dualist mould in a helpful way, yet drifts into a psychology in which the person evaporates entirely. I have called Part I From Personality to Social Psychology to underline the importance of the social constructionist critique in the understanding of people. This externalising moment sets the scene for Part II. Here I outline the alternative that I am proposing, tracing its roots and then showing how the issues and puzzles of personality look very different from its perspective. Here I call on phenomenology not only as a theoretical base, but also as a method, trying to engage the reader in imaginative variations and thought experiments (Ihde, 1986) to argue my points. I conclude by contending that the science of personality is both a practical and moral enterprise. Not only is understanding necessary in helping people to change and accept themselves, but it is something to which we *ought* to aim. The psychology of personality has to give up trying to be clever and explain people's behaviour. Yes, its job is to have a practical impact, but also to develop a vocabulary for moral reflection. In a world where tolerance is in short supply, the social scientist should interpret and speak for the marginalised, the foreign and the distressed.

One problem in trying to review so many different approaches in such a short space is that there is an ever-present danger of making straw men out of the opposition. Having said that understanding involves seeing things from the other's point of view, I felt bound to canvass the views of proponents of other positions as well as those of my own. I therefore submitted drafts of chapters to and discussed the ideas with friends who are psychoanalysts, social constructionists and therapists of different types. So I am indebted to Phil Salmon, Vic Sedlak, Ken Gergen, Peter Ashworth, Annika Gilljam and Angela Douglas for their very helpful comments. I would also like to acknowledge the strong support I have received from my friends and colleagues in the Centre for Constructions and Identity at the University of Huddersfield. This comprises sociologists and psychologists, a mixture of people and approaches without whom I could never have developed the view I elaborate here – in particular, Darren Langdridge, who tirelessly read and commented on various chapters; but also Viv Burr, Graham Gibbs, Dallas Cliff, Rudy van Kemenade, Jeff Hearn, Donna Gornall and Gary Fry all in different ways offered support throughout the project. All my contacts at Palgrave Macmillan, Frances Arnold, Andrew McAleer, Magenta Lampson, and Maggie Lythgoe have been a source of strong encouragement, and my partner June has been patient and understanding as I became more obsessed and absorbed with this project. I'm very grateful to Geoff Adams, who came to my aid in offering to construct the index just when I was running out of steam. Finally, I would like to thank the School of Human and Health Sciences Research Committee at the University of Huddersfield that made the whole thing practical by giving me sabbatical leave.

I won't say this work has been easy. Time and again I have remembered the wisdom of the late Douglas Adams: 'I can tell anyone how to write. You just sit in front of your Mac until blood comes out of your forehead.' But it has been enjoyable and, in retrospect, this has made it seem easier than it was. Since psychologists are fond of quantification, I could end this preface by saying that if you enjoy reading this book just half as much as I have enjoyed writing it, then I've enjoyed it twice as much as you. But I hope not. I hope you do enjoy it, and that it interests you enough to encourage you to find out more about the work of those theorists who in my view offer the best route to understanding people.

Trevor Butt
Huddersfield
November 2002

PART I

From Personality to Social Psychology

1

The Dimensions of Personality

Personality is perhaps the area in psychology that people connect with most easily. Most of academic psychology is concerned with processes – perception, cognition, development and learning. But the study of personality promises to put all these together to help us to understand individuals. We are fascinated with the behaviour of others and long to know why they act as they do. And we are frequently a puzzle to ourselves and want to know what 'makes us tick'. Why are people so different in what terrifies, excites and absorbs them? Why can't I keep to my diet, exercise regularly and generally keep all those new year's resolutions that embody such good intentions? And why do I find myself repeating patterns and mistakes in relationships that I know I should avoid? These are just the sort of questions that bring people to the study of psychology in the first place. And yet the psychology of personality frequently disappoints. Students find there are no simple answers. This is a pre-paradigmatic science in which there is no emergent consensus among academics, no agreement even about what units of analysis to focus on and how to approach them. We finish a course on personality and are still none the wiser about why I'm so anxious with people and she's not, how it is that some people can be so optimistic when I can't and what I have to do to exercise some self-control and restraint.

Now it may be that there are no simple answers and solutions – this certainly seems to be the case. But it is the contention of this book that in the project of understanding people, personality theorists have confused causes and reasons as well as prediction and understanding. Furthermore, the science of personality has largely and mistakenly confined its attention to what goes on 'inside' the person instead of examining the social context in which personal action arises. It is based on an assumption of Cartesian dualism: that we can separate mind from body and search for cognitions, constructs, traits and schemas 'inside' us to find the causes of behaviour. This is confounded by the assumption of another dualism of person–world, in which society is seen as external to the person and influencing in some way the interior life of individuals. In this chapter, I will first examine some of the issues that are addressed by personality theories, before returning to these problematic dichotomies and dualisms.

Personality is of course notoriously difficult to define. Any definition is tendentious, leading to the acceptance of some approaches rather than others. Harré (1976: 1) distinguishes between 'personality', 'character' and 'self'. 'Personality', with its derivation from the Greek *persona*, refers properly to our appearance to others, whereas things appear differently to actors themselves, providing us with a perspective of the 'self'. Underlying both perceptions is the actor's 'character', a source of behaviour, emotions and beliefs. Modern personality theorists tend to roll these three facets of the person together, emphasising some at the expense of others. Some concentrate on an objective study of behaviour while others stress the position of the self. The term 'character', with its pre-scientific flavour, has been excised altogether. However, a search for internal motives, whether this is in terms of source traits, cognitions or personal constructs, is very much at the heart of the personality project. Pervin and John (2001: 4) establish this working definition: 'Personality represents those characteristics of the person that account for consistent patterns of feeling, thinking and behaving.' They stress that 'as scientists we develop theories to help us observe and explain these regularities', and that we have to look inside the person for qualities that determine them. All reviewers of personality theories note a variety of related issues with which personality theories are concerned. While each text on personality differs slightly in what it sees as the main issues that a theory of personality should address, we can discern a set of issues that most would recognise as comprising the core of the project. I will briefly outline these below.

Issues in personality

The causes of behaviour

Following the model of the natural sciences, psychologists have sought laws that might govern behaviour. Indeed the concept 'behaviour' is one that belongs in the world of efficient causality. Aristotle had distinguished between different types of causality, but only efficient causes, where effects can be traced to direct environmental antecedents, were accepted in the post-Watsonian world of psychology. 'Behaviour' thus denotes something very different from 'action'. Behaviour is something a person is not in control of, whereas action is something that carries the intention of an intentional agent. We might ask agents the reasons for their actions, but not their behaviour, which is under the control of environmental stimuli and for which the agent cannot be held responsible in any simple way. But of course it is because everybody does not react in the exactly same manner to the same situation that the study of 'individual differences' had a place in a scientific psychology. Everybody brings to each situation a past that in some way influences what they do, whether we understand this in terms of pre-oedipal longings or a reinforcement history. Differences in biological temperament may also have their effect. And so theories of personality have wrestled with the relative effects of 'internal' and 'external' causality, nature and nurture, past and present in the production of behaviour. Of course it is rare to find a theorist who does not recognise the complexity of personality. Instead, there is an acknowledgement of an interaction in causality, and argument centres on the relative importance of the poles in these dichotomies. Nevertheless, this concession takes place in the context of a belief in efficient causality; to this extent nothing has changed and there has been no development of the basis of argument. In principle, it is assumed that if the scientist had full knowledge of all the relevant facts concerning history and biology, as well as a fine-grained description of the present environment, she could accurately predict a given person's behaviour in a given situation. Further research is always called for in order to establish factors controlling the regularities in behaviour. The issue of causality is particularly salient in two areas: the person's situation and her history.

The situation-specificity of behaviour

One particular dilemma for personality theories is the relative importance of the situation in governing what a person does. The concept of personality requires constancy of behaviour over time and in different situations. Yet clearly, situational context exercises some degree of control over us. On the one hand, we feel that we can recognise the signature of a person in any situation; what is particularly characteristic of her. Imagine that you are writing a reference for a friend. You naturally draw on traits to provide this. You might say that she is honest, hard-working and gets on well with others. This recognises what trait theorists propose; that people do vary in terms of traits, and when you label someone 'extraverted', you recognise a scale of introversion–extraversion along which people are ranged and are testifying that they are towards one end of the scale. You are also acknowledging a consistency that transcends situation. You are saying, in effect, 'I have found her extraverted, and I expect you will too'. But on the other hand, we have to concede that situations have a more or less strong effect in apparently determining behaviour. We do not need a personality inventory to explain behaviour at a red traffic light or understand why people take notes in lectures. Of course, occasionally, people will ignore a red light or talk throughout a lecture and then we might demand an explanation from them. But this only underlines those rules that structure social life, and that it is only when such rules are broken that we question how people act. The disturbing results of Milgram's famous obedience study (1963) remind us that the rules of the situation can all too easily produce behaviour that people would certainly regard as not characteristic of them. As I have already noted, we would not find any personality theorists who would deny both a consistency and a specificity in behaviour, and the literature talks of interaction effects between situation and person variables. It is the relative strength of these that is contended, against a background of an acceptance of some sort of causality.

The influence of the past

Theories of human development differ in how much weight they give to experiences in childhood in the formation of personality. It is sometimes assumed that psychoanalysis has a patent on the role of early experience. This is no doubt because, before Freud's publications in the late nineteenth century, it seems to have been assumed that children could be routinely abused (at least physically) without this having any effect in later life (Miller, 1985). Sadly, it has taken a century for this Freudian 'discovery' to work its way through, if only partially, into social life. However, it must be recognised that no personality theorist would deny some influence of the past, although there are disputes as to whether, for example, early experience always has more impact than recent events. The work on psychological trauma, and the widespread acceptance of post-traumatic stress disorder (PTSD), testifies to an acknowledgement that events in the world cannot be ignored. But just how we understand this influence is very important. Should we assume that some events, like sexual abuse in childhood, have an inevitable and predictable effect on the sufferer, or should we consider all impact as being mediated by some sense-making construction system that processes information and thus bestows meaning on it? As in the case of the effect of the situation, it is generally accepted that both event and construction matter, and an interaction effect between the two is proposed. But our understanding of the past and the status of our experience is not just a matter of academic debate. The practice of any psychological therapy depends on some theory of personality, some assumptions about the nature of humankind that guide the therapist's work – which aspects of personality is it realistic to attempt to change, and which must we accept and strive to come to terms with? A theory of personality should be able to tell us what it is realistic for us to expect; what we can reasonably aim at.

The relationship between cognition, behaviour and affect

This brings us to the problematic relationship between what we think, feel and do. Watson and others founded the first university department of experimental psychology in Chicago in 1914, breaking all ties with philosophy and sociology. In the wake of the behaviourism that he proclaimed, all talk of the causal effects of thought and affect were banished from the new scientific psychology. Erwin (1978) labelled Watson a 'metaphysical behaviourist'; one who simply did not accept the existence of thought. Subsequent behaviourists did not necessarily subscribe to this doctrine, and for a more interesting behaviourism we might turn to the radical and methodological behaviourism of Skinner (1974). Skinner claimed that mental events might be considered to exist – people talk a lot about their thoughts and feelings – but this was simply not of interest to a science of behaviour. This is because they are the product and never the cause of behaviour. Suppose someone insults us and we retaliate in some way. This is not because of feelings of anger and thoughts of revenge. It is the insult and the result of past reinforcing consequences that occasion our behaviour. The thoughts and feelings have the status of coefficients: they too occur as a result of the insult but, on their own, cause nothing.

Skinner would have disliked being called a 'personality theorist', insisting that there is nothing inside us like traits or complexes that have any value to psychology. Yet we can see that he was interested in the same questions with which the study of personality is concerned: the constancy of behaviour, the effect of the past and the relationship between thought, feeling and behaviour. For Skinner, 'personality change' meant behaviour change, and to change behaviour one had to build behaviour by modifying reinforcement contingencies. Until the mid-1970s, when the hegemony of behaviourism in academic psychology was displaced by the rise of cognitivism, both personality theory and social psychology had something of a parallel existence in the academy. The advent of a strong cognitive psychology revitalised the 'common-sense' view that thoughts and emotions did indeed cause behaviour. The encouragement of personal change now required an attack on all three fronts. Clinical psychologists, most of whom practised behaviour therapy, now embraced a cognitive-behavioural approach that was underwritten by cognitive social learning theory. The cognitive therapy developed by Beck (1976) and Ellis's rational emotive therapy (Ellis, 1975) were seen as being based on an information-processing approach and enthusiastically adopted by orthodox clinicans. Personal construct theory (Kelly, 1955) was interpreted as a psychology of personal cognitions (Ashworth, 2000). The characteristics of the person that account for consistent patterns of feeling, thinking and behaving were now seen as being essentially cognitive. Styles of thought, internalised dialogues, were held to produce emotional and behavioural responses. However, the primacy of affect was championed by Zajonc (1980), and a residual behaviourism argued for the primacy of behaviour. Once more, an interaction effect is proposed, with the balance of power in favour of a cognitive approach.

The sense of self

The concept of 'self' is a fuzzy and ill-defined one, used to refer to a number of related ideas. As one would expect, behaviourism had no use whatsoever for the concept. It was seen as the successor to the soul and the mind, an explanatory fiction that appeared to account for behaviour but in fact explained nothing at all. For Skinner (1974), the problem with a self was that the person was treated as a responsible agent and consequently the *real* causes of behaviour in the environment were ignored. In contrast, humanists like Rogers

(1951) attributed agency to the person. For them, people were self-directed agents, capable of transforming their lives and improving their circumstances. Furthermore, Rogers proposed that neurosis should be conceptualised as a failure of self-actualisation; a refusal to 'be oneself' in the face of social pressure.

Contemporary personality theorists do not align themselves along this dimension of behaviourism versus humanism. They neither endorse Skinner's rejection of dualism, nor Rogers' central position of the self in personality theory. Nonetheless, it is claimed that some reference to self-processes is essential to explaining personality. Pervin and John (2001) argue that some notion of self is necessary to explain, firstly, the integrity and unity of behaviour and, secondly, the observation that how we feel about ourselves influences how we process and act on information. The cognitive approaches to personality propose the existence of self-schemata and self-regulation systems that perform these functions. However illusory it may be, we have a sense of self and experience ourselves as having an integrity that transcends time and place. Concepts like 'self-esteem', 'self-efficacy' and indeed the 'self-concept' have been devised to denote self as a process within individuals and explain these phenomena. But if we conceptualise people as reflexive, self-regulating creatures, the status of 'behaviour' becomes problematic. Cognitive theories find themselves poised uneasily between seeing what we do as behaviour that is determined and purposeful action. And however they may wish to avoid it, they risk a return to dualism as well as a mentalistic psychology that methodological behaviourism fought so hard to avoid.

The influence of the unconscious

If the problems of conscious action are difficult to deal with, then the issue of unconscious feelings, cognitions and motivation presents even more of a challenge to theories of personality. We certainly cannot assume that all action is the result of conscious thought and deliberation. We are frequently puzzled by what we do, often regretting it and wishing we could exercise more self-control. If this is a feature of everyday life, it is most pronounced in so-called 'neurotic' behaviour. Now the concept of 'neurosis' is imported from a medical discourse that many psychologists find unacceptable. Nevertheless, psychoanalytic, humanistic and behaviourist theories all recognise a similar type of problem, even though they define it in quite different terms. Kovel (1976), a psychoanalyst, speaks of 'a lack of inner freedom', a sense of being driven. At the other end of the spectrum of personality theory, the behaviourists referred to the 'neurotic paradox', in which people behaved in ways that they disavowed. Here we find ourselves repeating problematic patterns of behaviour that are indeed characteristic of us. Clearly personality theory cannot ignore this phenomenon and it is in order to explain it that the unconscious has been called upon.

Psychoanalysis claims that conscious material is pushed into the unconscious through the process of repression, from where it remains a driving force. For this reason, it is referred to as a 'psychodynamic' approach to personality. Alternative theories may reject both the process of repression and the power of the unconscious. All the same, they have to reckon with the fact that characteristic patterns of behaviour occur without conscious control. Attribution theorists provided a wealth of experimental evidence of this (Ross and Nisbett, 1991) and cognitive psychology continues to elaborate areas of unconscious affect and cognition (Westen, 1998). Skinner (1974) provided a radical behaviourist account of repression, and Kelly (1955) made much of the construing that takes place 'beneath the level of awareness'. The way that we make sense of unconscious phenomena is crucial to our understanding of our lives. It is particularly important when we try to change ourselves or help others in their quest for personal change.

Implications for bringing about personal change

Among the major theories of personality, only trait theories have not addressed personal change as their central issue. It is no coincidence that most theories of personality have been generated and refined in clinical practice. It is in this context that all the issues above become most salient. Hans Eysenck, Walter Mischel, Carl Rogers, George Kelly and, of course, the psychoanalysts were all attempting to help people who were anxious, depressed or traumatised. Each had tried to help people to take hold of their lives in some way, to encourage personal change or self-acceptance. It was Kurt Lewin who was reputed to have said 'there is nothing as practical as a good theory'. We should expect theories of personality to have something useful to say about personal change; when it can be achieved, how to facilitate it and when it is impossible.

Psychological therapies are always based on some theory of the person, some model of human nature, and the variety of theories is reflected in the wide range of therapies available. Up until fifty years ago, psychoanalysis was unchallenged as the treatment of choice for neuroses, despite being beyond the reach of all except a rich and metropolitan minority. Its conception of neurotic complaints as 'symptoms' dictated that treatment should be aimed at unconscious causes rather than the symptoms themselves. Early behaviour therapists, by contrast, construed symptoms as behaviours, like any other, under the control of environmental stimuli and reinforcers. For Eysenck and Rackman (1965) the symptom *was* the neurosis; there was nothing beneath it to be cured. Skinnerians eschewed the term 'therapy' altogether, with its medical connotations and implications of underlying causes, and preferred the term 'behaviour modification'.

In the United States, Rogers (1951) mounted a different sort of critique of psychoanalysis, focusing on the therapeutic conditions that would allow the person to 'grow'. Drawing on the theory of self-actualisation, his proposition was that the therapist did not have to change anything, just remove the restrictions that had impeded psychological growth and development. The 'patient' of psychoanalysis and behaviour therapy became the 'client' of humanistic therapy; an active participant in, rather than a passive consumer of, therapy. Kelly's (1955) very different humanism saw the therapeutic relationship as one of research supervisor and research student (Bannister, 1983). This was built on Kelly's image of the 'person as scientist', again, very much an agent rather than a patient, but one who needed guiding in her life projects. As behaviour therapy 'went cognitive' in the mid-1970s, it was already moving to a more holistic conception of the person (Kanfer and Phillips, 1970; Eysenck, 1976). But the cognitive revolution, with its image of humankind modelled on the microcomputer, promoted information-processing theories of personality. Therapy was now cognitive-behavioural and aimed to modify cognitions directly, in the belief that behavioural and emotional change would follow.

So we can see that theories of personality have to do some work. Not only should they help us to understand both ourselves and others in everyday life, but also provide some guidelines about personal change. Will overcoming my shyness with certain people involve just learning some new habits, or will it necessarily involve a radical and 'deeper' restructuring? Can I overcome my depression by reasoning with myself, or will I need a therapist to help to examine my early attachments? Just *how* will I acquire the willpower to help me to stick to my diet? The evidence on the effectiveness of psychotherapy indicates that almost any type of therapy is successful with some problems in some people. For the past thirty years, researchers have focused on what sort of problems benefit from which type of therapy. The research has made some useful suggestions, but being able to predict does not imply understanding. Knowing that monosymptomatic phobias (that is, phobias with a single focus, say spiders, heights or needles) are often successfully treated with systematic desensitisation is not the same as knowing *why* this is the case. Theories of personality exist to provide explanation and understanding; why we are different from others, why we think, feel and act as we do and why change occurs. They propose widely different structures and processes to account for individual differences, yet they are alike in many ways. With the interesting exception of Skinner (who, as we have seen, would not regard himself as a personality theorist), they all hold dualist assumptions about the person, assuming an inner essence that makes its appearance through behaviour. In their search for explanation, they all stress causal relationships; some emphasise the power of situational variables, but most look inside the person for causal explanations. And they are all individualistic, assuming the existence of essentially separate individuals who predate the social world. These similar features can be seen as typical of modern scientific thought.

Personality: a modern concept

Let us now consider these points of similarity, examining the role of theory in the psychology of personality. One of the main purposes of theory in any field is to achieve understanding. Theories exist to help us to interpret and grasp the meaning of events. Scientific endeavour is characterised by the generation of theories that are designed to explain and make sense of different aspects of the world. This is part of the modern scientific project that dates back approximately three hundred years. The Enlightenment of the seventeenth century introduced what is termed the 'modern era' and challenged prevailing dogmas, subjecting them to scrutiny and empirical tests. Under the relentless experimental programme that subsequently developed, nature gave up more and more of its secrets as humankind subjected its environment to research, bending it increasingly to its control.

The success of this scientific project is clear enough. We have machines that have made things much easier, we have ventured into space and we enjoy an extended life expectancy. One only has to imagine living before the invention of anaesthetics to appreciate the improvement in the quality of life for people. So it is not surprising that such high status is now attached to science. To be scientific is to be at the cutting edge of knowledge, predicting and controlling events in the world that were previously assumed to be out of our reach. Whereas philosophy is seen as essentially passive, an armchair practice that changes nothing, science is about active intervention. When John Watson established the first university department of experimental psychology in Chicago nearly a hundred years ago, he broke away from the department of philosophy. Philosophical inquiry came to stand for everything that psychology rejected and contrasted itself with. Above all, it centred on objective dispassionate inquiry. Introductory texts in psychology frequently contrast the objectivity of early behaviourism with the hopeless subjectivity of introspection, decried as 'armchair philosophy' in which the pre-scientific gentleman/philosopher apparently attempted to describe the contents of his 'mind'. In contrast, behaviourists restricted their data to what could be observed, to behaviour that could be objec-tively defined.

I have already pointed out that the study of personality has its roots not in the experimental tradition, but in parallel develop-ments in early scientific psychology. These were the development of psychometrics on the one hand and clinical psychology on the other. Even so, personality theorists insisted on the scientific nature of their work. Personality questionnaires were called 'objective tests', and theorists like Eysenck (1953) were keen to distance themselves from pre-scientific modes of inquiry. In the 1970s, however, impor-tant changes occurred in the experimental approach to psychology. The behaviourism that focused on rats and pigeons was displaced by a cognitive psychology that in many ways rehabilitated the 'mind', that set of inner workings that could not be observed directly, but inferred from verbal and non-verbal behaviour. Information-processing models of the mind became increasingly important, not only in the explicitly cognitive personality theories, but also to back up trait theories. Modern science searches for causal explanations beneath surface appearances and thus personality theories have sought expla-nations in cognitive and, to some extent, neurological terms. In this there is always a danger of reductionism, that is, explaining by re-course to a more molecular level and not capturing the complexity of the phenomena we are attempting to explain. There is also the danger of what Skinner (1974) called 'explanatory fiction', inventing an imaginary homunculus that works the person. This is the issue of dualism.

Dualism

The notion of a soul that inhabited the body was a part of ancient Greek thought that became incorporated into Christian philosophy. This, along with other aspects of Christian dogma, remained unchallenged in Europe until the Renaissance. Then, in the early seventeenth century, Galileo's new scientific approach questioned the received dogma, subjecting it to scrutiny and rational critique. Descartes, the seventeenth-century mathematician and philosopher, was impressed by the Galilean revolution in scientific thinking whereby mechanical causes for phenomena were considered the only real explanations of them. But, as a religious man, he was reluctant to jettison the idea of the soul that inhabited the body. He wrestled with this problem, focusing on how one can be misled by one's senses as the opening one has onto the physical world. Looking for a fixed point, ground on which one can stand and be certain of, he reasoned that while the public physical world is always open to doubt, what cannot be doubted was the position from which one doubted – one's thought. This leads to the oft-quoted Cartesian conclusion: *Cogito, ergo sum* (I think, therefore I am). His solution to this problem was to propose that the mind and body comprise different substances, what Ryle (1949) called the 'doctrine of the ghost in the machine'. It accepted that the body, being part of the material world, was subject to mechanical laws, while the mind was not. But the mind still had the power to cause bodily behaviour, being responsible for our purposeful and intentional action. Ryle sums up the properties of this spectral agency:

> Though the human body is an engine, it is not quite an ordinary engine, since some of its workings are governed by another engine inside it – this interior governor-engine being one of a very special sort. It is invisible, inaudible and it has no size or weight. It cannot be taken to bits and the laws it obeys are not those known to ordinary engineers. Nothing is known of how it governs the bodily engine. (Ryle, 1949: 21)

The Cartesian distinction between mind and matter promoted the acceptance of psychology as a separate discipline. Biology might be expected to explain the physical aspects of the body, which was subject to material laws, but psychology was intended to understand this 'interior governor-engine', with its special and mysterious relation to the body that housed it.

Causal relations

The psychology of personality has inherited many Cartesian assumptions, with many theories looking inside the person in order to explain her behaviour. The concept of 'motivation' was invented in order to discover factors which 'energise and direct behaviour'. It assumes that the body is basically an inert substance, lying at rest until it is kick-started by some motive force. In the Cartesian system, the body belongs to the material world and is subject to physical and biological laws. The mind, on the other hand, pulls the body's strings and works its will through some causal network that it is the purpose of personality theories to explain. Whether we conceive of these connections in terms of unconscious motives, efficacy beliefs, self-schema or traits, the personality project is aimed at the explanation of surface behaviour in terms of underlying forces.

However, it would be wrong to imply that personality theorists have been satisfied with a dualism that passes responsibility for behaviour to an invisible inner person. Modern science has triumphed by taking things apart to see how they work, moving from the molar to the molecular level in search of satisfactory causal explanations. Traits, cognitions and unconscious forces are sometimes seen as partial explanations only, to be explained in their turn through the discovery of the neurological networks that constitute them. This is 'reductionism', the seeking of explanations at a more molecular level than that at which the things to be explained occur. It is not a principle with which all personality theorists are comfortable. Many would see it as an exercise not in explaining, but explaining away, personality phenomena. Nevertheless, the growth in popularity and prestige of brain science testifies to its power on both the academic community and the public generally, and it still preserves the idea of a ghost in the machine. In this reductionist version, the ghost is exorcised; proved to be a superstition belonging to a pre-scientific age. The body is conceived as a machine still, but not the crude clockwork type that Descartes envisaged; instead it is like a computer, the sort of complex machine that was unimaginable in the seventeenth century.

Individualism

Individualism is a doctrine that is so pervasive in the modern world that we have difficulty in seeing it at all. Rather like water to the fish, it is only visible to the relatively distant observer. We can attempt to achieve this distance by examining the contrasting world views of other cultures and other eras which do not share our individualistic assumptions. Of course we are all biological individuals, units that are indivisible and separate from each other. There is a private world of sensation within each of our skins. I cannot feel your pain and you cannot sense my tiredness. But the doctrine of individualism claims that we are also psychological individuals. In this possessive individualism, it is assumed that each person contains within them their own traits, feelings, motives, attitudes and thoughts. We can see here how this assumption seems axiomatic to us today, and especially to psychologists. The sort of things inside people provides us with a list of topics around which psychologists have organised their discipline. As such, it is a corollary of Cartesian dualism. Descartes privileged mind over matter; as we have seen, his fixed point was the *cogito*, the thinking mind that cannot be doubted. In this sphere of privacy, the person is in direct contact with the mind's contents, whereas the body, along with other aspects of the material world, can only be known through the medium of potentially misleading senses. Descartes claimed that feelings, thoughts and motives were transparent to our inner gaze, but, since Freud, we have come to think that, for one reason or another, we might deceive ourselves about them. At the beginning of the twenty-first century, contemporary folk wisdom encourages us to get in touch with our feelings, as well as to be, to know and even to find ourselves. The tenets of possessive individualism seem unquestionable. We assume that feelings, emotions, thoughts and motives exist to be discovered. And where else could they be, but inside us?

But there is a second dualism that follows in the wake of the mind–body: that of person–society. Each person is a container of her inner private world and outside the boundary of the skin is both the physical and social environment. The self is inside and society is outside. The psychological individual is then elevated into a position of primacy. This individual, it is claimed, is concrete, real for all to see, while society is an abstraction. Psychology studies individuals, while sociology focuses on society. In my view, this way of dividing up the field is highly problematic, as we will see in subsequent chapters. Psychology has moulded itself after the high-prestige natural sciences, whereas sociology is merely a social science. No one disputes that society is made up of individuals and that individuals exist in the context of society. But individualism claims that, in an important sense, individuals precede society. Social psychology, that aspect of psychological science that deals with the social world, generally sees individuals as atoms that come together to produce and determine sociological phenomena. It acknowledges the existence of conformity, groupthink and obedience to authority, but sees these as puzzles to be explained primarily at the level of the individual.

Understanding people

In this book, we are interested in what it means to understand people, ourselves as well as others. We have noted that the study of personality should surely be where we should look in psychology to help us in this quest. After all, personality is that area of psychology concerned with individual differences and the role of theory is to provide explanations. We have seen that there is little agreement about how to conceptualise the person. Nevertheless, theories recognise similar issues in personality and share dualist and individualist foundations in their search for causal explanations. So is there any possibility of a consensus about what makes people 'tick'? Now, some theorists would say that understanding individuals is not the job of a personality theory. I remember seeing Hans Eysenck speak, when a member of the audience said: 'I have an E score of 12 and an N score of 11: so do millions of others, so what does this tell you about me?' Eysenck replied that there was nothing in the world like his favourite pair of slippers. What could a scientist say about them? Well, if you put them on a fire they'll burn, and if you were to drop them, they wouldn't break. Similarly, a science of personality 'understands' people, in the sense that it indicates how they will behave in certain well-defined circumstances. It isn't concerned with a detailed account of individuals. This answer defines understanding in terms of prediction and is the sort of response that binds the psychology of personality firmly to the natural sciences' project of prediction and control.

In the natural sciences, understanding has become synonymous with prediction. This is because control of the natural world has been the aim of the game of natural science. Now this might have a place in psychology. We want to know how to guard against mindless obedience, how to shape the environment to encourage pro-social behaviour and who will benefit from a particular type of therapy. The sort of knowledge we acquire here is relevant to populations rather than to individuals. It tells us that, generally, people with this type of E score have these sorts of psychological disturbance, and that people with these sorts of belief generally benefit from this type of therapy. But this should not be the only objectives of a psychology of personality. With its focus in psychotherapy, personality theories ought to have something to say about particular individuals. We legitimately want to know why some people benefit from social skills training while others don't, and exactly who will get something out of it. Understanding involves more than mere prediction.

Toulmin (1961) gives us a good example of how prediction need not involve any understanding. He tells us that the ancient Babylonians were able to predict accurately astronomical events, for example lunar eclipses. This was due to their careful study of repeated patterns that were apparent in the heavens. But they had no understanding of what the moon and stars were, the difference between stars and planets and why the regularity in patterns occurred. They tried unsuccessfully to extend their forecasting to other natural phenomena, like earthquakes and plagues. No theoretical speculation accompanied the accuracy in forecasting. The Ionians, on the other hand, could predict nothing successfully but came up with a variety of primitive explanations about stellar motion. Nowadays, Toulmin points out, we expect both prediction and explanation from a scientific theory. But theories do not always give us new predictions. The tides could be accurately predicted long before Newton's theories explained them and Newtonian physics did not add to the sailor's practical knowledge. In the natural sciences, a satisfactory explanation is causal: it tells us what forces are in play and how they interact to produce particular effects in the natural world.

I want to question this definition of understanding and argue for a version of understanding that is quite different. The type of understanding I will be advocating is not new, it has been around in the social sciences for at least a hundred years. It can be labelled as *verstehen* or 'hermeneutic understanding' and was a current of German thought that was imported into the social sciences in the late nineteenth century (Outhwaite, 1975). Weber, Dilthey and Simmell are the theorists most often associated with it. In Continental Europe, it was important in the development of both gestalt psychology and existential phenomenology. In the USA, it influenced the course of

American pragmatism through George Mead, who was a stud_
of Dilthey's in Berlin in 1900. The interpretive sociology of the Chicago School can be traced back to Mead, as can aspects of Kelly's
psychology of personal constructs. Hermeneutic understanding does
not look beneath or behind phenomena in order to explain them; it
does not take things to pieces in order to see how they work. Instead,
it makes sense of them by contextualising them. This is rather like
making sense of a piece in a jigsaw puzzle; we look to see how it fits
into a larger pattern. Understanding properly involves what Dilthey
(1988) saw as a 'hermeneutic circle': moving from part to whole and
back to part again in order to see how things fit together.

This is like understanding what someone is saying. We make sense
of what is said by understanding the relationship between words in a
sentence and of sentences within a still broader social context. The
sentence is the structure that gives a meaning to the word that we
would miss if we just looked it up in a dictionary. So when someone
says 'Oh, I'm pleased to see you decided to turn up', we know that
'turn up' has nothing to do with her performing a somersault.
'Turn' is in itself ambiguous, but there is nothing ambiguous about
the way in which it is used here; the context clarifies the meaning.
But the actual meaning of the sentence only becomes clear when we
can place it in the context of what else is happening, and the context
of convention and social practice within which this is embedded.
So, if we are thirty minutes late for an appointment, we might conclude that what was said was not meant literally. Such an understanding then requires an appreciation of what an appointment is,
as well as a grasp of the uses of irony. So understanding involves a
to-and-fro cycling between parts and whole to make sense of what
is meant. Dilthey saw this type of understanding as most relevant in
the social sciences and contrasted it with the type of reductionist
explanation favoured by natural scientists. Understanding people
is like understanding a text. It is not like explaining the movement
of particles.

Now, if we decide that an appreciation of social context is vital in
understanding people, we might have to rethink the relationship between personality and social psychology. This branch of psychology
is concerned with how people 'perceive, comprehend and interpret
the social world' (Aronson et al., 2002). Indeed, it is often puzzling
to new students of psychology just how social psychologists and personality theorists have carved up the psychological territory between

them. Attitudes, dispositional attribution and person perception are areas in social psychology that all have parallel existences in personality theory. And in the English-speaking world, social psychology has been dominated by a cognitive approach, focusing on how individuals construe their social environment. However, in the last twenty years, assumptions of dualism, individualism and causality have been questioned by social constructionism. This is a family of approaches characterised by a rejection of the modern scientific approach to the person, with its search for an internal essence that precedes the social world. It stresses the contingent nature of the person, laying particular emphasis on the role of language in the construction of individuals. I will elaborate these points in Chapter 4, but briefly, social constructionism holds that rather than developing from the inside out, so to speak, the person is formed by societal structures. Language is a particularly important social structure, in that it both facilitates and restricts not only what we say and write, but what we can think about. In surprising ways, it is possible to see similarities between social constructionism and Skinner's radical behaviourism. Both doctrines reject the notion of an internal reality that manifests itself in a person's behaviour, and would therefore deny any involvement in the study of personality. Personality to both is an invention designed to make individuals assume an impossible agency. It is to either environmental contingencies (for Skinner) or social structure (for the constructionists) that we should look for the causes of behaviour.

In the following chapters, I will firstly review approaches to personality, looking at how they conceptualise the causes of behaviour and underlining their individualism and dualism. Then I will examine social constructionism, to see what this missing approach to personality has to offer. I will argue that while personality theories overemphasise personal agency, social constructionism underplays it: that the person dissolves altogether in the tide of social structure. I will then turn to hermeneutic understanding, contending that an existential phenomenological approach to personality gives us a more fruitful way of understanding people. And finally, I will revisit the issues in personality that I have outlined above, saying how this approach offers us a different way of conceptualising personality and personal change.

2

Personality Theories 1: Trait, Biological and Cognitive Social Approaches

In this chapter, I want to begin reviewing contemporary personality theories. Clearly, in so little space, I can only attempt a brief sketch of each. But my aim is not to give a comprehensive description and critique of these theories, instead it is to examine their (sometimes implicit) assumptions about the person; what is sometimes referred to as their 'philosophical view'. I want to look at the frequently invisible foundations behind personality theories, and I will argue that a belief in dualism, mechanistic causes and individualism make up these foundations. The first problem facing anyone trying to review these theories is how to group them. Different texts on personality use related although slightly different categories. I will divide the field into four: trait and biological, cognitive social, psychodynamic and humanistic. In this chapter, I will look at trait and biological and cognitive social theories. I will review these together because they have had most impact on orthodox academic psychology. They have developed mainly in the psychometric and experimental traditions respectively. By contrast, the psychoanalytic and humanistic theories that I will look at in Chapter 3 are embedded firmly in the clinical tradition. Focusing as they do on individual experience, they are more open to phenomenological interpretation. In contrast, trait and biological and cognitive social theories follow the traditional natural scientific approach to the accumulation of knowledge.

Trait and biological approaches

A trait can be defined as any relatively enduring way in which one individual differs from another. Trait theories are the most convenient way to begin discussing personality, because they most resemble lay theories. If someone asks for our opinion of someone else, we naturally sum him up in terms of traits. For example, we might say that someone is prickly, slow, sensitive or too dependent. Each of these descriptions has implications of behavioural stability. We are saying that we would expect that you will find this person as we have found him – it is not that his sensitivity is just a function of the situation in which he might find himself. There is also the implication of dimensionality. Contemporary trait theorists are not claiming that we either have a trait or that we lack it. Theirs is a nomothetic approach to personality, emphasising dimensions along which all people can be seen to vary. And in our everyday description, we are implying that others, in contrast, are not prickly or are less dependent.

Trait theorists see this connection with common sense and usage as a strength. They claim that the fact that we use trait terms in everyday life indicates their utility. Why would trait descriptions be so pervasive and extensive if people had not found them useful in predicting the behaviour of others? They believe that this folk psychology tells of traits that lie behind and indeed determine behaviour. Furthermore, they demonstrate that trait usage transcends culture, and argue that this points to constitutional and biological factors that are indicated through personality traits. Everyday trait usage is therefore where this approach starts from, and the 'psycholexical approach' begins with everyday terms, looking at how people rate others on trait dimensions. However, one problem is that it has been estimated that there are 18,000 words in the English language that could be thought of as trait terms. This obviously includes many synonyms, and it is also thought that some clusters of traits tend to go together. So trait theorists have had to refine this extensive list down to a manageable description of the person. For this they have relied on the statistical technique of factor analysis, a method of correlation that clusters and groups traits in an economic yet (it is claimed) meaningful manner. Clearly there is a delicate balance to be achieved here. The more economic the description, the less it captures the individuality of the person, but the more idiosyncratic and fine-grained the analysis, the less is our ability to compare one individual to another.

Much of the dispute within the trait theory community has centred on this issue. Cattell (1965) argued that it made most psychological sense to describe individuals in terms of the sixteen personality factors that he identified and developed in his 16PF inventory. These correspond to 'source traits' that worked away beneath the level of 'surface traits' to determine them and, through them, an individual's specific responses. Eysenck (1953) preferred to work at a higher level of abstraction. He pointed out that the sixteen factors were not independent of each other and that they, in turn, could be reduced to two higher order factorial dimensions: extraversion (E) and neuroticism (N). He later added a third: psychoticism (P). Those who preferred to work at the level of sixteen factors did not dispute the mathematical validity of this operation, but they did question its psychological validity. They believed that it was useful to describe individuals at this level. The 16PF inventory could be used (and indeed still is) by occupational psychologists to screen people for jobs, predicting which individuals are best suited to particular employment. The Eysenckians' reply was that the higher order factors made most psychological as well as mathematical sense. To begin with, they were more reliable and stable. This means that you are more likely to achieve similar scores on repeated measures on two factors than sixteen. Also, and from a psychological perspective more importantly, N and E scores predicted both the likelihood of psychiatric breakdown and the form that it might take. A high N score does not indicate neuroticism per se, but predicts that, under stress, you are more likely to suffer psychological disorder than someone who has the good fortune to have a low N score. Somebody with a high E score is likely to develop more hysterical symptoms, whereas somebody with a low E score is more likely to become anxious or depressed. In the last decade there has been an attempt to integrate these two approaches around a nucleus of five bipolar trait dimensions (Goldberg, 1992; Costa and McCrea, 1992). These 'big five' factors are extraversion, neuroticism, agreeableness, conscientiousness and openness to experience. However, the big five solution has impressed neither Eysenck nor Cattell, and there is no consensus about the number of factors that most appropriately describes personality.

Traits as descriptions and explanations

I referred to description above advisedly. Critics of trait theory have long noted that as they stand, traits do not explain behaviour.

Skinner (1974) saw all mentalistic terms like traits as explanatory fictions: descriptions of behaviour that masquerade as explanations. When we say that Emma likes parties because she's sociable, it sounds at first as though we've provided some sort of explanation. She is an extravert and one of the main features of extraversion is sociability. But all we have really done is identify a regularity in her behaviour. This is typical of Emma, who likes things such as parties, nights in the pub and meeting new people. We might guess that if she completed an Eysenck Personality Inventory, she would gain a high E score. But extraversion here does not explain her liking of parties, it simply describes it. We could perhaps more accurately say that we call her sociable *because* she likes parties and similar events. As Skinner would insist, this is surely the logical way round to see things. He theorised that we should look for the real causes of behaviour not inside people, but in the contingencies of reinforcement that they have been subject to, along with the discriminative stimuli that occasion operant behaviour. To rely on what Skinner called 'mental way stations' is to indulge in a cycle of redescription and not to explain phenomena. He argued that people are strongly encouraged to subscribe to the myth that behaviour can be explained by mental events. This is because, in an individualistic social climate like ours, society (or, as Skinner preferred to call it, the verbal community) wants people to accept individual responsibility for their behaviour.

This type of pseudo-explanation is quite common in both psychiatry and everyday life. Szasz (1970) declared that mental illness was a myth partly on the grounds that psychiatrists invoke diagnoses in just this way. To call someone schizophrenic, he contended, is not to explain their behaviour but simply to redescribe it and note that it fits into a pattern, in effect, a cluster of traits. Of course, psychiatric diagnoses are not personality traits. Nevertheless, some trait theorists like Eyesenck (1953) see their dimensional model as replacing psychiatric categories, and claim that psychiatric disorders are in fact trait clusters in an extreme and maladaptive form. As we have already noted, in describing others in everyday life, we usually do so in terms of traits that they apparently possess, and this is used as evidence of validity for the trait approach. But this undeniable everyday practice does not necessarily mean that we are using traits as explanations. It usually constitutes advice about how to interact with people. When we say that someone is aggressive, we are saying 'be careful' and when we say someone else is trustworthy, we are saying perhaps that it's OK to confide in them. We are not interested in *why* they're like they are; explanation is just not necessary in order to follow a rule. For the scientist, however, explanation is important, and trait theorists see traits as determining behaviour. Mischel (1968) commented that whether traits are conceptualised as cognitive entities or hypothetical constructs, they have to do more work than merely redescribing behaviour at a trait level. Traits themselves still have to be explained.

The biological basis of behaviour

In order to provide an explanatory basis for traits, theorists have turned to neurology and biology. The relationship between biologically determined temperament and personality has always been emphasised by trait theorists. Eysenck pointed to the observations about personality types of Galen over 2000 years ago to argue that biologically driven aspects of personality transcend time and society. With their pre-scientific outlook, the ancient Greeks thought typology was due to the balance of humours in the body. Contemporary trait theorists look not to humours but to neurotransmitters in the brain to explain personality. Their research suggests that the big five are underpinned by neurotransmitter balance in the central nervous system (CNS). But from now on, I want to concentrate mainly on Eysenck's theory. This is for two reasons. Firstly, alone among the trait theorists, Eysenck was primarily concerned with behaviour change. His work began with a clinical focus and not in occupational psychology. Secondly, his theorising (Eysenck, 1967) provides a good example of the linking of traits to a biological basis of behaviour.

Eysenck (1967) argued that one reason for the stability of his second-order personality factors (and the relative instability of the sixteen first-order source traits) was that there was a sound biological basis for extraversion and neuroticism. His evidence for this claim came from a body of research that showed correlations between these two factors and a variety of perceptual phenomena and learning tasks. So, for example, extraversion is related to vigilance decrement, critical flicker-fusion threshold and classical conditioning. He reasoned that this must be due to individual differences in brain functioning and suggested that extraversion is related to cortical arousal, while neuroticism is related to autonomic arousal. Cortical arousal refers to the general level of a person's arousal, ranging from hyper-alertness to slumber. Apparently, people differ in their 'default' setting on this range, being normally distributed along it.

Eysenck showed a correlation here with extraversion; people with a high E score were those who were habitually in a state of low cortical arousal (as evidenced by the learning and perceptual tasks). The extravert, then, is relatively 'stimulus-hungry', when compared to the introvert. Perhaps introverts are quiet and retiring because they are bombarded by the environment in a way that extraverts are not? For whatever reason, Eysenck (1967) contended, the personality dimension that we construe as extraversion–introversion is caused by individual differences in cortical arousal. Both are normally distributed functions. But the cortical arousal is the genotype, the underlying cause, while the behaviour is the phenotype, the appearance that reflects the underlying differences in brain function. In this case, the brain functioning lies in the brain stem, in a collection of neurones known as the 'ascending reticular activating system' (ARAS). This system regulates the general level of activation in the cerebral cortex, providing a background of alertness against which specific stimuli are dealt with.

In a similar way, neuroticism is caused by differences in autonomic arousal. The autonomic nervous system is that branch of the central nervous system that controls involuntary activity like heart rate and respiration rate. This is the system that looks after our fight-or-flight mechanism; our ability to react speedily in a crisis. It is subject to classical conditioning, adapting to situations that herald danger. According to Eysenck, people differ in the extent to which they are generally autonomically aroused. Some 'fire up' very quickly and take longer to return to a resting state than others. Those people also score highly on the neuroticism scale of the EPI. Again, this is a normally distributed function, determined by individual differences in the brain's limbic system. I commented earlier on the 'good fortune' of having a low N score, and that is just what it is: good luck. Eysenck asserted that what we think of as personality is a biological function, largely genetically determined. All the same, he was not pessimistic about behaviour change. Our constitutional temperament might act as a limit to our abilities, but there is no doubt that environmental contingencies have an important effect. Contemporary theorists no longer see things in terms of nature versus nurture, but of nature *and* nurture. Most people diagnosed as neurotic have a low E and a high N score. For Eysenck, who strongly championed conditioning theories and early behaviour therapy, this showed a link between conditioning and temperament/personality.

Trait theory and reductionism

Trait theorists have been keen to ground their work in neuro-physiology, avoiding the criticism that traits simply redescribe behaviour. They see a basis in neurology as supplying the explanation of behaviour that is required by theory. It also avoids the problems of dualism, which passes responsibility to the ghost in the machine and instead provides a materialist account of behaviour. Now the thesis of this book is monist, and I want to develop an understanding of people that is based in monism rather than dualism. But trait theory is reductionist and represents a crude form of monism. Here, psychological phenomena are reduced to a physiological level of explanation. Minds are reduced to brains and particular cocktails of neurotransmitters in them. There are two types of problem with such reductionist explanations, one empirical and one conceptual.

The empirical problems are to do with evidence that contradicts the conclusions. In reductionism, explanations are one way: neurophysiological facts explain psychological facts, not vice versa. But biological psychologists are much more cautious about reductionism than trait theorists. They point to correlations between neurophysiological and psychological phenomena, but do not infer cause. Toates (2001) reviews a number of studies showing the ambiguity and reciprocal nature of causality in this area. Certainly an excess of noradrenalin is associated with anxiety and dopamine with feelings of pleasure. Drugs that increase the level of serotonin in the synapses of the CNS sometimes alleviate depression. However, this does not show that neurotransmitters cause mood states. A high blood level of the hormone testosterone is associated with competitive, aggressive and dominant behaviour. But this does not mean that it causes anything. Neurotransmitter levels are constantly in flux. Aspirin relieves headaches, but no one suggests that headaches are caused by a lack of it. And experiments have shown that competitive activity produces high levels of testosterone. In many ways, trait theory is built on confusion between correlation and cause. The evidence for the very existence of traits rests on correlations that show very little variance in common between items on a personality test but are statistically significant (Mischel, 1968). And the existence of a biological basis for traits depends on a one-way causal direction for which there is no empirical support.

This brings us to the conceptual problems. These are to do with the shaky logic behind reductionism in the social sciences. In the natural sciences, success has come from looking to more micro-levels to explain phenomena. So, before the invention of microscopes, the disease processes occurring at the level of the cell were not understood. Infections might wrongly be attributed to being overexposed to the night air, a curse or bad luck. The identification of bacteria led to a new realm of scientific explanation. A reduction to the chemical level led to yet further understanding, for example about the inheritance of disease. Explanation here hinged on the structure of DNA, an organic acid that exists in the chromosomes within the nuclei of cells. This all works because cells are made up of chemicals (and these in turn are made up of molecules and atoms). In the social sciences this logic has led to individualism; society is made up of individuals, and psychology is the science behind sociology. It has also led to the idea that neurophysiology is the science behind psychology, because individuals are constituted as people by the brain. We might think that we can explain traits, supposed regularities in behaviour, by recourse, say, to the prevalence of neurotransmitters. But the behavioural level and the physiological level are not different realms. It is not possible logically to explain events at one level by recourse to the other. They are different ways of talking about the same thing. Crossley sums this up very nicely by referring to them as 'different discursive registers' (Crossley, 2001: 22). It must be emphasised that this is definitely not a return to dualism. It is what Kelly called 'constructive alternativism', the taking up of a different perspective on the same event; construing the same thing differently. (See Chapter 3 for a more extensive discussion of Kelly's theory.) Our bodies are equipped to experience wavelengths in a particular range as colour, and vibrations with a particular range as sound. But experience is not explained by talking about wavelengths and vibrations. These are physicists' ways of talking about the physical world.

So when we say that someone is anxious, it cannot be explained by saying this is due to noradrenalin. Neither can high noradrenalin levels in the body be explained by feelings of anxiety. Perhaps the feelings we identify as anxiety are the experiential equivalent of the physiological description. But certainly no one could look at blood hormone levels and say 'this person was anxious'. Schacter and Singer (1962) demonstrated that blood noradrenalin was necessary but not sufficient to explain experienced emotions. The same chemical could power other similar emotions. Similarly, no neurologist could point to a brain cell or neural network and say 'this person was thinking about his dinner'. The misconception of interaction between brain and mind states occurs when we flip from one level to the other, as though they refer to different things and not different constructions of the same thing.

Cognitive social approaches

Cognitive social approaches to personality have taken firm root in academic psychology in the last twenty-five years. This followed a devastating attack on trait theory from the social learning theorists. The vast majority of clinical psychologists in the UK now explicitly or implicitly subscribe to a cognitive social conception of personality. It provides the rationale behind psychological therapies that are broadly cognitive-behavioural (Ellis, 1975; Beck, 1976; Dryden, 1987). Mischel (1987), one of the principal theorists in this field, notes how the cognitive revolution in psychology quickly had an impact on academic, developmental and social psychology. It was, however, resisted by conservative forces in the field of personality that clustered, as he sees it, in three camps comprising trait, psychodynamic and behavioural theorists respectively. Mischel (1993) argues that the theories of both Rogers and Kelly (see Chapter 3) were the first rebellion against these orthodoxies, but being seen as confined to clinical psychology made them easy to marginalise in the academy. This rebellion came to a head in the late 1960s, crystallising around Mischel's (1968) attack on trait theory and Bandura's (1969) on radical behaviourism.

The critique of traits

I first read Mischel's *Personality and Assessment* (1968) when I was a clinical psychology student in the early 1970s. At that time, British clinical psychologists were still psychometric testers, routinely and often pointlessly administering intelligence and personality tests in a futile effort to help psychiatrists to allot their patients to unreliable psychiatric categories. It always used to remind me of the *Monty Python* sketch where two people are comparing astrological descriptions. One reads out hers and says something like 'You are a ten-foot long green man-eating crocodile with glasses. There you are! They were right about the glasses!' A psychiatrist could read a personality description, select bits that confirmed his opinion and say how sensitive the instrument was. Clinical psychologists wanted to make a difference and most saw behaviour therapy as a way of doing this. Mischel's critique of the concept of the trait, along with his advocacy of a cognitive-behavioural understanding of people, was more than welcome to a new generation of clinicians.

His contention was that there was very little evidence for the consistency in behaviour that traits supposedly represent. We think of ourselves as being consistent across time and in different situations. There is plenty of evidence, however, that behaviour is much more situation-specific that we imagine. There are also many accounts of people changing as they mature and undergo new experiences. This is hard to explain if we hold a trait theory based on deterministic biological temperament. Of course, trait theorists recognise the effects of mood and situation, but still maintain the existence of underlying consistency in the form of personality traits. Their reply to Mischel's argument was that the evidence for traits comes from their standardised objective tests. But Mischel (1968) pointed out that the only standardised and objective aspect of a personality inventory is in its administration and scoring. Everyone does the same test in the same standardised conditions and the scoring is done with a stencil and is therefore free of tester bias. But when it comes to filling in an inventory, we are asked to make subjective judgements and vast generalisations. For example, we might be asked if we like parties or often have headaches. We might want to say: 'well it depends on what type of party and who's there' and 'what does "often" mean?' But there is no room for this clarification. We are asked to work as quickly as possible and not reflect on our answers. 'Objective' should mean keeping a diary, when we might find that we liked parties less often that we'd thought, and that 'often' is in fact only twice in the last fortnight.

As we have seen, trait theorists point to the use of traits in everyday interactions, insisting that this reflects an underlying real consistency that we see in ourselves and others. In the construction of their tests, they extend this process, getting thousands people to rate others they know, and on this basis distil factors that are the basis of their theories. But Mischel (1968) pointed out that the traits might reflect the personal constructs and prejudices of the people doing the rating, and not those being rated. Traits, like beauty, may be in the eye of the beholder. He cited one study in which people rated others who they saw for a few minutes and had no opportunity to interact with. The same stable clusters of traits appeared that are used to rate people that were known well. This clearly suggests that people readily assign traits to others on the basis of no real evidence. We read in attributes that aren't really there and also make unjustified assumptions about traits going together. The social psychological literature on attribution shows, for example, that once we have decided someone is a 'warm' person, we go on to assume with no evidence at all that he is also trustworthy and generous. Further evidence for Mischel's position comes from experimental work on the 'fundamental attribution error' (Ross and Nisbett, 1991; Van Boven et al., 1999). This focuses on the fact that observers regularly make dispositional rather than situational attributions when assessing the causes of another's behaviour. Dispositions are what personality theorists would label either 'traits' (enduring characteristics of the person) or 'states' (transient moods or emotions). Even when observers are warned that they must take the situational context into account, they overemphasise dispositional factors.

Mischel's conclusion was that the so-called objective tests used by trait theorists in fact tap into a culturally shared trait theory as well as individuals' self-concepts. So, a person might indeed see himself as an extravert and think that this explains his social activity. But all we get from a personality test, Mischel claimed, are self-concepts and personal constructs. If that is what is really being assessed in personality inventories, we should use measures that are specifically designed for the purpose, like the repertory grid (Kelly, 1955). All this does not mean that Mischel advocated a totally situation-specific view of behaviour. He did not deny the behavioural signature that each individual has, but argued that this is not captured by trait theory. Instead he contended that we need a cognitive process theory, one that spelt out the idiosyncratic meaning of situations to individuals. Our behaviour will be consistent across time and situations to the extent that we construe situations as similar and expect certain consequences to flow from our action. At first glance, this appears to resemble a Skinnerian position of analysing behaviour in terms of discriminative stimuli and reinforcers, but, of course, Skinner would never have used such cognitive terms.

The critique of behaviourism

Behaviourists like Skinner promoted a deterministic view of the person in which the behaviour of people is, in principle at least, entirely predictable in terms of the situation and their history of reinforcement. The social learning theorists, by contrast, believe that the person is an active processor of information, constructing meaning and acting in the light of his interpretation of events. Bandura (1969) exhaustively reviewed the role of awareness in learning, showing its importance in understanding behaviour. Awareness, he argued, was not an epiphenomenon, just a superfluous froth collected on the real substance of behaviour. It was essential to understand the person's individual meanings and hypotheses in order to make sense of what he was doing. This is very different from behaviourist accounts of awareness, in which people are in more or less the same position as observers, watching their own behaviour and drawing conclusions from it. The real action goes on beneath conscious awareness, and is caused by the contingencies of reinforcement. Of course, we all have privileged information about ourselves; we have sensations about pain and tiredness that are not publicly available, but otherwise, we are just like others watching and inferring motives and causes of our behaviour (Bem, 1972). This passive account of the person was rejected by the social learning theorists, who see people as modelled on microcomputers, essentially information-processors that generate meaning.

This view has important implications for explaining learning. The behaviourists had relied on conditioning theories that required no cognitive mediation. A phobia was explained in terms of classical and operant conditioning (Eysenck and Rachman, 1965). This required a traumatic pairing of a neutral stimulus (say, a spider) with a stimulus that naturally produced fear and shock (say, a loud noise to an infant). Escape and later avoidance of the newly conditioned stimulus (the spider) then drove home the conditioning. Neuroses were seen as examples of maladaptive learning (for Eysenck, this process was most likely to occur with introverted neurotics). But even those who had once promoted this theory came to recognise its shortcomings (Rackman, 1980). Most phobics do not give traumatic accounts of their problem, and many exposed to traumatic conditioning do not develop phobias. Also, one would predict that there would be many people terrified of things like machinery, which are often responsible for injury, and few terrified of spiders, which (in the UK at least) injure nobody. But in fact, the reverse is the case. So, how do people come to be phobic of small animals? It was argued that, as a species, we appear to be biologically prepared to make some associations, presumably due to some evolutionary advantage of rapidly learning to respect potential threat. But not everybody is scared of snakes and spiders.

Bandura (1969) had demonstrated that probably the best way to overcome fears is through participant modelling. This is where we watch a model, say, pick up a snake and overcome their apprehension. We then copy them. Surely, if people overcome fears in this way, perhaps this is how they are acquired in the first place? In a series of experiments, the social learning theorists showed the importance of both modelling and vicarious reinforcement (the process where we learn by observing what happens to others). They emphasised how this 'no response learning' required cognitive mediation, arguing that observation gives people information. How they act in the light of this depends on expectancy based on reinforcement history. So it was concluded that learning is cognitively mediated and not stamped in automatically by the environment. Bandura (1977) argued that effective therapy of whatever type always worked through a final common pathway: the modification of efficacy beliefs. In everyday language, we can translate this as confidence – the belief that you can do something that will be effective. While participant modelling was often the best source of these beliefs, they might also be changed through several other methods.

This work had an impact on the practice of clinical psychology and the development of psychological therapies. Up until the mid-1970s, behaviour therapy had been seen in orthodox psychology as the only therapy with proper scientific credentials. Now the challenge was to modify cognitions directly, and both cognitive therapy (Beck, 1976, 1991) and rational emotive therapy (Ellis, 1975; Dryden, 1987) were included in a new cognitive-behavioural family.

The person in cognitive social theories

An information-processing model

The emphasis on cognitive processes, along with the critique of traits, leads to the question of the status of the person in cognitive social approaches. Mischel dealt with this with reference to what he called 'person variables' (Mischel, 1973), and later 'cognitive affective units' (Mischel and Schoda, 1995). He proposes that people differ in terms of encoding strategies, expectancies and beliefs, affective response, goals and values and self-control strategies. Just imagine you are with a friend, Tom, who gets into a pub brawl. You can't imagine why he did, but he says he was provoked by Bill. He interpreted

Bill's look as a challenge and felt angry. For him, the most important thing is not to be 'pushed around', and he says he's always had a short fuse. You didn't see Bill as being difficult and even if he was, it wouldn't have mattered to you. Anyway, you've always had better control of your temper than Tom has. Here we see differences in a range of psychological processes that come together and explain why people differ so much. For Mischel, this wouldn't be captured by ratings on a trait of aggression. Unless Tom is provoked, he's perfectly placid, and it's only a very special type of circumstance that provokes him. You, on the other hand, might be much more aggressive on the sports field, in political debate and competition at work. Mischel and Schoda (1995) claim that the 'if ... then' structure of their information-processing approach is much more appropriate to understanding personality. We could predict how Bill would act *if* someone acts in a particular way, which is likely to challenge and infuriate him. *Then*, he is likely to hit out and never mind the consequences.

The move from 'variables' to 'units' is important, as it is claimed to be an advance in scientific understanding. Mischel and Schoda (1995) refer to networks of neurological connections to back up this move. Hebb (1949) had speculated about the existence of cell assemblies that in many ways has been developed and elaborated in the contemporary work on neural networks. Here, assemblies of cells become connected, in the sense that synaptic transmission between them is facilitated by repeated firing. So associations develop which result in repeated feelings or behaviour patterns. The importing of this idea into personality theory promises an eventual reductionist understanding. For the social learning theorists, there is a reciprocal determinism between the person and the environment. In principle, we could eventually predict someone's behaviour if we had all the relevant neurological knowledge, plus a description of his situation. There is the tantalising promise that mysterious and puzzling responses will one day be explained. This is because, in the end, this is a deterministic approach; it is the firing of neurones, over which we have no control, that controls the person's action.

Cognitive social approaches to the person are underwritten by the concept of information processing, and see the person as a sophisticated microcomputer. Although they use the modern scientific vocabulary of cognition, affect and behaviour, they retain the Cartesian distinction between mind and body, giving a privileged place to cognition. The family of cognitive-behavioural therapies has been admirably pragmatic, using a broad-spectrum approach that attempts to modify cognition, affect and behaviour (see, for example, Lazarus, 1987). Nevertheless, in the end, this is a rationalistic group of therapies. Its advocates believe that the 'elegant' way to achieve change is through rational dispute and Socratic dialogue (Ellis, 1975; Beck, 1976). The way we feel and act is caused by our cognitive structure. People frequently consult therapists because, in some way or other, they feel bad about themselves. A very common complaint in young adults is of social anxiety; feeling anxious with other people. Some feel shy in the presence of attractive others and students often dread giving a presentation. They describe themselves as hopeless and lacking in confidence. In the heyday of behaviour therapy, this common-sense formulation would be reversed: 'It is not beliefs and feelings about yourself that cause you to act in a socially clumsy way, but seeing yourself acting like this that causes negative self-attributions.' In social skills training (Argyle et al., 1974), behaviour was shaped and reinforced in the hope that clients' confidence would increase. Nowadays, a cognitive-behavioural regime would address not only clients' behaviour, but also their beliefs directly. Indeed, therapists would put beliefs about the self at the centre of their strategy.

The work of Markus (1977) on self-schemas can be seen as providing experimental support for this new emphasis in therapy. Arguing against the radical behaviourist view prevalent in the early 1970s, she contended that we consider the self as a set of cognitive schemas. These were described as bipolar constructs such as confident–timid. Information about the self is filtered by these schemas and processed accordingly. Information that confirms the self-schema is likely to be accepted, while counter-schematic information is not. So, if I think I'm a hopeless at giving presentations, I'm likely to see evidence to the contrary as insignificant, and focus instead on the one example when I made an absolute fool of myself. This idea fits in nicely with Beck's (1976) proposition of negative monitoring in depressives, where the client only notes bad occurrences. Markus (1977) showed how people readily processed and accessed information about themselves that was consistent with their self-schema. So, if you see yourself as very timid, you collect examples that demonstrate it and remember such examples easily. Counter-schematic information is resisted. So, I'll dismiss examples of my social confidence as one-off and atypical. Her work on 'possible selves' extended this idea (Markus and Nurius, 1986). In this, it was argued that people would exhibit inbuilt resistance to self-development in some directions. This is where we find ourselves developing in ways that imply counter-schematic representations. On the other hand, we each have several possible selves that we could develop, where this elaboration is not blocked.

The image of science

This work of Markus is deservedly well known and recognised in the psychological community. But what is interesting is that parallel theoretical developments in personal construct theory (Kelly, 1955) are not. This is interesting because, I believe, it says something about what pychologists think science is. Mischel was a student of Kelly's, and readily acknowledged the pioneering nature of his work on personal constructs. I will describe Kelly's work in some detail in Chapter 3, but will say something very briefly about it here. Kelly proposed that we think of people as like scientists, each with their own theories about the world and, most importantly, about themselves. The self here becomes a theory, a set of bipolar personal constructs (like confident–timid!). In a contribution to a symposium on motivation, Kelly (1969a) addressed the 'neurotic paradox' in which people find themselves acting in self-defeating ways. He proposed that self-elaboration depends on the articulation of this construct system. Choice is effectively blocked in some directions. We can see here the parallels with the work of Markus and her colleagues. While Kelly used the term 'self-theory', Markus used the cognitive vocabulary of schema. Pervin and John (2001) also note the similarity. But they see the information-processing approach as a scientific advance in two ways. Firstly, they believe it shows how cognitions are related to action and motivation. Markus explained how what people do and say is related to what they think. Secondly, it enabled personality work to be placed in a broader cognitive context. Thus it can be communicated to and appreciated by the wider psychological community.

In the first of these points, we can see the strong strand of dualism that underpins cognitive psychology and, through it, social cognitive approaches to personality. The early behaviourists derided cognitivism as leaving the person 'lost in thought', a charge that still apparently rankles today. Describing how people think, imagine and feel is one thing. Showing how this converts into action is another. How does the ghost pull the levers of the machine? The mental and material realms are separate, made up of distinct substances and not just different discursive registers. Kelly's theory was seen as purely cognitive, indeed bloodless; critics claimed that there was no room even for emotions in it. Motivation was that branch of psychology that was meant to explain just how the person was kick-started into action and Kelly (1969a) would have no truck with the concept. Explanation and understanding in the field of personality means an ever-more fine-grained analysis of the interface between mind and body, leading eventually, it is hoped, to an understanding of the 'interaction' between them. The contention of this book is that this represents a misunderstanding of the status of mind–body, which are not separate sets of events, but separate constructions of the same events. As such, it is a completely futile scientific quest. We might as well search for how the elements of air, fire, earth and water contribute to the making of the soul.

The second point reflects Pervin and John's (2001) observation that a cognitive paradigm is becoming dominant in psychology. In the development of a mature science, there is a move from a pre-paradigmatic phase, in which a variety of perspectives contest the ground with each other, to a paradigmatic phase in which there is a growing dominance of a single perspective. Their evidence for this comes from a study they cite carried out by Robins et al. (1999). These authors surveyed publications in the most prestigious mainstream psychological journals in the last three decades. They showed an ascendancy of articles drawing on a cognitive perspective in this period. The strength of an information-processing approach to personality is that it fits in with this trend, allowing constructive dialogue with other psychologists and a growing understanding of a range of psychological phenomena. But the 'flagship' publications examined by Robins et al. are mainly North American. There is clearly a danger here of mistaking a cultural hegemony with an international consensus. What about the journals published in France, China and Russia? Perhaps the possessive individualism inherent in America has influenced what seems like an acceptable framework to psychologists there? People possess motives, cognitions and emotions much as they possess cars, mobile phones and houses. An individual responsibility is a corollary of this view, and we look inside people to cognitive structures in order to modify their behaviour. Another way of interpreting the data of Robins et al. (1999) would be that it shows that it is difficult to be published in high-status American journals unless you subscribe to a cognitive perspective. Any psychologist hoping to get an article published in a high-status journal had first better translate it into cognitive vocabulary.

But perhaps this is unfair, and the firm grip that cognitivism holds in American academic psychology flows from its theoretical power. I have already referred to the quote attributed to Lewin: 'There is nothing as useful as a good theory.' A powerful theory has to have some useful applications. Each theory has what Kelly (1955) termed a 'focus of convenience', an area in which it must have particular use. Cognitive social approaches to personality are supposed to have informed the practice of cognitive-behavioural therapy. But I don't think they have a convincing case here. I think that influence in the reverse direction is more important; it is the success of the cognitive therapies that has strengthened a cognitive approach to personality. Beck and Ellis were conducting their therapies for twenty years before they were 'discovered' by cognitive psychologists. Both originally trained as psychoanalysts and were used to working in a pragmatic way, drawing on whatever proved useful to them. (It is interesting that Beck *does* draw on Kelly, advocating his model of the therapeutic relationship.) Beck and Ellis were enthusiastically drawn into orthodox psychology, finding, as it were, that they had been 'talking cognitive-behavioural prose' all their lives. But it is difficult to think of any great discoveries from the work of cognitive social personality theorists that have informed therapeutic practice.

Kelly (1969b) disputed the view that there is a 'pure' laboratory-based psychology and an 'applied' psychology in the clinical field that applies the principles discovered by the pure scientists. If anything, he claimed, it is psychotherapy that is 'pure', in that in this endeavour we have the chance to see people making important life decisions and wrestling with the difficulties of the human condition. Academic psychologists are fond of calling Freud's work 'pre-scientific'. They ask how we can legitimately generalise from a sample of neurotic Viennese women who lived at the turn of the twentieth century. Of course, there appeared to be no problem in generalising from rats, pigeons and the American college students who inhabited psychological laboratories! But Kelly argued that, in psychotherapy, we do not see extraordinary people, but people at extraordinary moments in their lives. And real moments too, not those artificially concocted by the experimenter. In searching for psychological principles he could use in therapy, Kelly (1969c) found nothing in the academic psychology of his day. But he drew on Freud's writing; there, he claimed you could see someone contending with real issues and dilemmas. But the myth of a pure and an applied psychology is still very much with us today. I have already mentioned Mischel's comment that early dissent with trait theory was easy to marginalise because it was located primarily in the clinical field. Nevertheless, important approaches to personality have been generated there, and it is to these that we will turn in the next chapter.

3

Personality Theories 2: Psychoanalytic and Humanistic Approaches

Whereas the approaches discussed in the last chapter have their origins in the academy, the two I will be considering here have their roots firmly in the practice of psychotherapy. Trait and biological theories came out of the psychometric tradition, while the cognitive social learning theories were developed in the experimental tradition. On the other hand, psychoanalytic and humanistic theories come from and are still clearly located in the clinical tradition. As we have seen, cognitive social learning theories are related to the practice of cognitive-behavioural therapy. But proponents of these theories cling to a pure/applied distinction, in which the therapy is seen as an application of the pure science. Even so, I have argued that there is a good case that can be made for this traffic to be seen as mainly in the other direction: that the theory's main support comes from the so-called application. But cognitive-behavioural therapists also differ from both psychoanalysts and humanistic psychotherapists in that their focus is on specific cognitions and behaviours (Beck, 1976). Psychotherapists working in the Freudian, Rogerian and Kellian traditions would see behaviour change as intertwined with personal change generally. For them, any enduring change in the person therefore requires an understanding of the person in a more comprehensive sense. Perhaps because the theories to be discussed in this chapter have their focus in the understanding of individual clients, they are more open to a phenomenological interpretation.

Phenomenology is concerned with how things appear to people, and this is clearly vital when we are trying to help people to accept or change aspects of themselves. Nevertheless they are frequently interpreted within a natural science framework.

Psychoanalysis

The term 'psychoanalysis' has two interrelated referents: a theory of human development and personality, and a method of psychotherapy based on this theory. Both originated in the work of Freud. In this chapter, we will focus on the theory of personality, but this will involve some consideration of the therapy, since this nicely illustrates important aspects of the theory. Psychoanalysis is the most misrepresented of all personality theories, with most textbooks only dealing with the writings of Freud, and giving no consideration whatever to developments that have taken place since his death in 1938. Westen (1998: 334), reviewing the evidence from contemporary psychology for analytic propositions, comments that it is all too easy to dismiss psychoanalysis when you focus exclusively on Freud: 'To reject psychodynamic thinking because Freud's instinct theory or his view of women is dated is like rejecting modern physics because Newton did not understand relativity.' Westen points out that the most exciting development in psychoanalytic thinking in the last thirty years is object relations theory (ORT), and that this rarely receives even a mention in texts on personality. Now, it is important to review ORT for two reasons. Firstly, it has dominated British psychoanalytic thinking since the 1920s. Secondly, Symington (1986), a noted British psychoanalyst, detects two quite different currents in Freud's thinking: a mechanistic determinism and a hermeneutic understanding. While ego psychology represents the first, ORT embodies the second of these. Ego psychology continues the developments in analysis introduced by Freud's daughter Anna, and has taken strong root in the USA. This, perhaps, is why we only read about this variant in psychology texts. So, I will begin by reviewing Freud's theory, emphasising aspects of it not often picked up in orthodox personality texts, before considering ORT.

Freud

It is important to understand Freud's thinking by contextualising it. He was very much a product of the Enlightenment; a humanistic atheist working in medicine in the last days of the Austro-Hungarian Empire. Symington (1986) tells us that he was strongly influenced by the Physicalist Society, a group of prestigious doctors who believed in mechanistic and organic causes for all disease, including mental illnesses. Freud's training was as a neurologist at a time when it was hoped and expected that neurological causes would be discovered for the neuroses. Indeed we can see that this is embodied in the common root of both terms. The mechanistic determinism of the Physicalist Society left no room for agency or intentionality on the part of the person, and Freud never relinquished his desire for a scientific respectability that was predicated on this approach. Nevertheless, he developed a hermeneutic approach to therapy, in which the aim was to make interpretations to the patient that would enhance agency and choice. The aim of psychoanalytic therapy was to help people become less driven and at the mercy of unconscious forces, and the analytic credo was 'Where there was id, there shall be ego.' Curiously, his concurrent use of these entirely contradictory metapsychologies is seen as a strength by some commentators (for example, Ricoeur, 1970).

In his early work, originally written in 1895 (Breuer and Freud, 1956), he attempted to trace the origins of hysteria. This is a condition in which people exhibit neurological-type symptoms, such as paralysis or blindness, for which there is no neurological cause. At first, he concluded that it was sexual trauma that caused hysteria. The hysterical women he treated reported childhood sexual abuse. The mental pain of the trauma had been unconsciously converted into physical pain. This is how the concept of, and hence the term, 'conversion hysteria' originated. A hundred years later, many psychotherapists (for example, Miller, 1985) believe that sexual abuse is indeed the cause of many neuroses, but in 1897, Freud became more cautious. Several factors (including his own self-analysis) underlined for him the impossiblity of separating fact from fantasy, and led to him proposing an Oedipus complex in young children. This refers to a child's sexual desire for her mother, which Freud believed was a normal attachment, later to be repressed. There is nothing abnormal or problematic in repression; it is one of the prices that humankind pays for living in civilised societies. But various resolutions of the process do lead to solutions that are very costly indeed, and these we see in neuroses. Here we can see two of the controversial ideas that are associated with Freud: the existence of unconscious mental processes and childhood sexuality. Symington (1986) points out that neither originated with Freud. The idea of an unconscious had been around for about a hundred and fifty years, and the sexuality of children was already accepted by sexologists such as Havelock Ellis.

Freud's division of mental life into conscious and unconscious processes is referred to as the 'topographical model'. It is particularly important to distinguish between preconscious and unconscious phenomena. All personality theorists would accept the existence of preconscious processes. Our sensory systems simply could not cope with the vast array of stimulation we are subject to, and we rapidly habituate to a variety of sensations that it is not important for us to attend to. The colour of the walls, the sound of distant traffic, the smell of garden flowers as well as a vast range of proprioceptive and kinaesthetic sensations all vie with each other for our limited attention. But any aspect of this preconscious material could be focused on by the searchlight of consciousness if it became vital to do so. For Freud, dynamically unconscious material is quite different. It has been repressed; forced into unconsciousness from where it cannot be voluntarily retrieved. A boy cannot afford to remember his love for his mother and his resultant envy and hatred for his father that was so difficult for him at the age of four. The bitter lesson of the father's superior power and his mother's attraction to him is something he has adaptively put out of his mind. So this is a dynamic unconscious and the material in it is there as the result of a process of repression. Freud's attraction to mechanistic causes is evident in his proposition that for material to become conscious, energy has to be expended, and that this is withheld in the case of repressed material. He believed that, in time, scientists would be able to discover the neurological systems at work in the topographical model.

The early topographical model was gradually replaced in Freud's thinking by the structural model. In the *Ego and the Id* (1962), he developed and elaborated the well-known concepts of 'id', 'ego' and 'superego'. Although it is tempting to think of these as cognitive entities, it is interesting to note that in the German language in which Freud wrote, he did not use these Latin terms. Instead he used ordinary German words that translate literally as 'I', 'it' and 'over-I'. The Latin names in the English translation make us think of mental structure in a way that the use of non-technical terms do not. It is possible to think of this not as a structural but a phenomenological model, a way of describing a person's experience. One way of reading it is to see it as elaborating ways in which people can feel as though their thoughts, feelings and actions are not truly theirs. We feel overcome by passion, by an infatuation or hatred that wells up inside us in a way we are ashamed of. Our experience is that 'it', something we are not in control of, is determining our action. We might say we were 'overcome' by emotion or 'out of control' of ourselves. We deny agency and responsibility, yet it was undoubtedly us that felt and did these things. In this way, Freud was saying that we are divided beings, ruled by different principles. The id is in the service of the pleasure principle (and the death drive); it wants gratification of biological needs. The ego that develops out of the id has to serve reality and mediate between the demands of the id, the inhibitions and threats that emanate from the superego and the reality of the social world.

Freud saw the superego, that internal regulating voice, as a function that grew out of the oedipal conflict. It is sometimes translated into everyday language as a conscience, but this doesn't convey the hard persecutory tone that analysts see as characteristic of it. They see it as one source of human aggression, where people project their persecution onto convenient others. But Freud placed more emphasis on aggression in his later work. Following his disillusion with 'civilised' society following World War I, he postulated a death instinct that he saw as responsible for humankind's destructive impulses. It is this aspect of his thought that was taken up by Melanie Klein.

Object relations theory

Klein

There are two people who are historically associated with the advent of ORT, Melanie Klein and Ronald Fairbairn. Klein had moved to London in the 1920s, and strongly influenced the analytic community there with her pioneering analysis of children and her theories of the mental life of the infant. Although Freud had concentrated on the oedipal period, and the neuroses that were the supposed consequences of it, Klein (1932) stressed the importance of the pre-oedipal period. Here, the focus is not on the three-person relationships of the oedipal period, but the two-person mother–child bond (although Klein also posited the existence of an early oedipal situation). The strange term 'object' refers to the object of libidinal energy, and reminds us of Freud's mechanistic energy theory. The infant's object is eventually the mother but, initially, it is the 'part-object' of the mother's breast, her smell or touch. Before the infant has relationships with the whole person, she has relations with these part-objects, which are not coordinated into a gestalt of person – this comes later. Klein stressed the inner life of the infant, which becomes populated with these internalised or introjected part-objects and the infant's relationships towards them. And these can be characteristically good or bad. Our objects can frequently be experienced as frustrating or punitive, as well as nourishing and supportive. All this, of course, takes place at an unconscious level. The infant does not have language with which to spell out her feelings or articulate an inner conversation. Nevertheless, she is primarily in relation, albeit of a non-verbal, feeling kind.

All psychodynamic theories propose that patterns of relationship become initiated in early childhood, have an unconscious base and tend to repeat themselves, often in a puzzling and distressing way in adult life. For these approaches, personality is a product of early relationships and unconscious phantasy. This is not captured in the superficial rational and biological approaches of orthodox personality theory. Since psychoanalysis is a clinically based enterprise, it has focused on personality problems, and for the Kleinians, it is our maladaptive object relations that haunt us and result in psychological disorder. Klein elaborated Freud's notion of a death instinct in order to account for the prevalence of bad object relationships. This is where psychoanalysis differs from other personality theories in its proposition about basic human nature. For the cognitive-behaviourists, people are essentially rational, whereas for Rogers (to be discussed later) they are essentially good. Both Freud and Klein stress that a person's split nature will contain the capacity to love and the wish to destroy and hate. In common with all the monotheistic religions – Judaism, Christianity and Islam – they propose a state of original sin from which people have to be rescued. Klein emphasised the natural envy, hatred and greed of the infant. She believed that when we hate our objects, we experience our objects as hating us. When our internal world is full of phantasies of damage and revenge (Kleinians use the term 'phantasy' to denote unconscious fantasy), we see the external world as correspondingly threatening and live fearful lives. We can see this is a far cry from the simple conditioning and efficacy belief models of the cognitive-behaviourists! For psychoanalysts, obsessional, phobic or hypochondriacal personalities are the products of unconscious projections. As a result of these early part-object relationships, the infant adopts a 'paranoid-schizoid position'. This is characterised, as we have seen, by a paranoid world view, and also an internal splitting (hence 'schizoid') that is undertaken to protect the infant from a damaging set of object relationships.

What can save the person from adopting this position in later life is care that helps the infant to manage this inner turmoil. Klein made much of a process termed 'projective identification' that has its roots in the mother–child relationship and is the basis for empathy. In projective identification, we have a phantasy of projecting our feelings into others and making them experience our anger or our terror (and we often behave in ways that indeed elicit these responses in others). This might sound a bit crazy, but an examination of our everyday experience shows something like it is commonplace. We often find another's mood is contagious, or that just being with a jolly friend cheers us up and conjures up a different side of ourselves. We meet people who produce a strong atmosphere or aura around them, and who seem to dictate what we can or cannot say without any overt instruction. For the Kleinians, these are all examples of projective identification, which is first used by the infant to communicate wordlessly with her mother. The mother feels the baby's distress, frustration and anger – she doesn't infer it from her behaviour, but experiences it directly. The 'good-enough mother' is one who doesn't give a knee-jerk response and instead contains and holds these feelings, applying her mind in order to detoxify them so that the infant too can manage them. If the caretaker isn't overwhelmed, then neither is the infant. In psychoanalytic therapy the analyst works principally with 'transference' and 'countertransference' phenomena. Here, the patient–therapist relationship is seen primarily in terms of feelings that are projected between analyst and patient. Personality is conceived in terms of characteristic patterns of object relationships that have their origin in infancy and repeat in current relationships both inside and outside the therapy room.

Fairbairn

Fairbairn's (1952) take on ORT was slightly different from that of Klein (1932). It developed in parallel and had no reference to innate destructiveness and the death instinct. In Britain, three psychoanalytic groups evolved, each with their separate training programmes: the Kleinians, the Classical Freudians who followed Freud's daughter Anna, and the Independents. This last group drew on Klein's work, but has been most strongly influenced by Fairbairn. He broke completely with Freud's early mechanism and the attendant concept of libidinal energy that seeks discharge. Libido, for Fairbairn, was object-seeking and not pleasure-seeking. This formulation stresses that it is the relationship with 'objects' that is paramount and that psychological disturbance occurs in the wake of unsatisfactory or pathological relationships. The ego is not a development of the id; not a structure set up to negotiate between the demands of energy discharge and the realities of social life. Instead a pristine ego precedes the id. The implications of this are important. It means that interaction with significant others precedes the individual and that one's inner life is not made up of innate quanta of energy, but forms in the context of social interaction. There is no notion of original sin here. The infant is born willing to be pleased, so to speak. The paranoid-schizoid position is a response to traumatic disappointment with one's objects. It is then that she turns away from the world of true object relations and becomes consumed with internal bad objects. This means that she carries forward from childhood a pattern of poor relating to significant people. People find themselves recreating bad relationships. This is clearly unconscious, in the sense that they do not do this in a deliberate, thought-out way. Nevertheless, it is they who are doing it, albeit in an unconsciously intentional manner. So, for example, Lucy might find herself excited by and at the same time drawn to men who use and then reject her. It might be obvious to her friends that this is going to end in another disaster, and indeed that she invites rejection. 'There she goes again', they might say. From a psychoanalytic perspective, the explanation is to be sought in the way she related to her mother and/or father, or other early objects of attachment.

This stress on the infant's early environment led the Independents to emphasise the importance of good mothering. Of course, this can never be perfect, and Winnicott (1971) coined the phrase 'good-enough mothering'. Developing to the mature dependence of adulthood means being able to accept disappointment. Nevertheless, the responsibility for psychological health rests with the caretaker. Bowlby's work, so often completely misrepresented in psychology books, was carried out in this tradition. It argued against Klein's proposition of innate destructiveness, and for the environmentalist view that insecure attachment resulted from the child's experience that her objects could not be relied upon. A secure base with secure attachments was essential to healthy psychological development. This view has important implications for how a psychoanalytic treatment is conducted. For the Kleinians, there is an inevitable focus on the negative transference. Psychological change can only come about when people recognise their own destructiveness, and this begins in the therapeutic relationship. The patient's projections onto the analyst, say, for example, as a cold and persecutory figure, must be analysed. This is not necessary and might indeed be harmful if the main aim of analysis is to encounter the analyst as a person, not merely as a figure on whom to project transferences. Fairbairn stressed the restorative aspects of the therapeutic relationship. The analyst seeks first of all to create a situation that is conducive to the development of transference relationships. When Lucy acts in a flirtatious and later in a sulky way, the analyst might comment on this, linking it to the excitement/rejection cycle already noted. The aim of the analyst would be not to participate in the cycle and survive the attack that might follow. In this way, Lucy has a chance to deliberate on what she is doing and perhaps work towards changing it, first with the analyst and eventually with her boyfriends. Symington (1986) argues that this restorative function of therapy, in which the client may learn new ways of object-relating, is reminiscent of the formulations of the neo-Freudians like Jung and Adler. In some ways it is also similar to that of the humanists.

Humanistic approaches

What characterises humanistic approaches is that they hold that people are conscious agents who make choices and are not driven by forces, either external (like reinforcing contingencies) or internal (like a dynamic unconscious). This is why they insist on calling people in therapy 'clients' rather than 'patients'. The word 'patient' refers to someone who is suffering passively and this is why it is used widely in medicine. There is no element of choice, conscious or unconscious, with the patient with asthma, cancer or influenza. But to call people in psychotherapy 'patients' is, for the humanists, misleading. This is because it denies people's freedom and responsibility for their action. Certainly clients suffer, but to call them patients is misleading.

It has to be said that there was also a political reason for talking of 'clients'. In the USA, the medical profession had (and still has) a very firm grip on the conducting of any therapy. In Britain, most psychoanalysts are now not psychiatrists, but in the USA, you had to be medically qualified to become an analyst when Rogers was practising. Medicine has always had a very strong influence on psychoanalysis, and this is one reason why it is resistant to a phenom-enological reading and insists on the use of a vocabulary replete with pathology. Even in Britain, it used to be the case that your path as an analyst was much smoother if you had medical training. Both Fair-bairn and Bion (who was one of the most intellectual Kleinians) were extraordinarily educated men with first degrees in the humanities. Both found it necessary to train as doctors however. When Carl Rogers was practising over forty years ago in the USA, he had to invent the term 'counselling' to describe what he was doing; psychol-ogists like him couldn't do therapy. The talk of clients rather than patients further differentiated his style of practice from psycho-analysis. Kelly talked of patients as well as clients, and uses the term 'therapy' rather than counselling. One wonders if perhaps he wanted to distance himself from the work of Rogers as well as from other types of psychology. As we will see, they are very different types of humanism. I will analyse Kelly's approach in more detail than that of Rogers'. This is for two reasons. Firstly, he set out his theory more explicitly as a formal theory of personality. Secondly, while both his and Rogers' theories can be readily interpreted phenomenologically, Kelly's is often taken to be a species of cognitivism and is hence more ambiguous. It is therefore more interesting for the purposes of this book, particularly because, in my view, it offers a more convincing phenomenology than does Rogers'.

Rogers' person-centred theory

Rogers (1980) described his approach to personality as resulting from his experiences in his life generally, but particularly in his role as a psychotherapist. He recounted how as a shy young man from a fundamentalist Christian home, he was changed through his encoun-ter with the woman he later married. In a similar manner, he con-cluded that in therapy, personal change occurred not because of the practising of some technique or other, but as a consequence of a deep and genuine human encounter between therapist and client. Effec-tive therapy is not likely to occur when the therapist is perceived as being cold, phoney or distant. When the therapist is warm, empathic and genuine, however, the climate is such that the client is able to grow and develop. It is important to note the organic metaphor here. 'Growth' is a term that we apply to the maturational process; seeds grow into plants and children grow into adults. And this is very much Rogers' view about people. He recalled how he saw a barrel of

potatoes in the cellar of his parental home. In the darkness and lacking nourishment, their growth was hindered. But they still did what
potatoes did, even in these adverse conditions – they sought out any
light and grew towards it. Misshapen and handicapped, they still
attempted to develop into the plants they had the potential to be.
Humans, Rogers believed, had a similar actualising tendency. Each
of us has the potential to develop in a particular way, but few of us are
in the soil or the other growth conditions that promote such growth
and self-actualisation. The neurotic is like the potato forced to grow
in the dark, producing a perverted form of growth.

We can see immediately that this is a very different picture of
humankind from that of Melanie Klein. Client-centred therapy consequently has to focus not on the analysis of resistance and not on the
recognition of innate destructiveness, but on allowing conditions of
growth. Rogers' early version of therapy was consequently called
'non-directive therapy'. The therapist's job was to interfere as little
as possible and simply to reflect clients' feelings back to them. Later,
he acknowledged the subtle reinforcement contingencies in play in
any encounter and called his approach 'client-centred therapy'.
The promotion to a 'person-centred approach' reflected his asser-
tion that these therapeutic principles obviously have application in
society generally and not just in the therapy room. In child-rearing,
education and social life in general, Rogers advocated the same principles of non-interference with individual growth.

Indeed, Rogers believed that neurosis was the result of societal
interference and pressure. It was the expectations of others – parents,
teachers and society in general – that prevented individuals' self-
actualisation. In our attempt to conform to social norms, we fashion
a false self, denying an inner real self that, left to its own devices, would
grow in a natural way. The neurotic is like the potato in the dark;
forced into an unnatural perverted form. His theory allowed for
preconscious adoption of defence mechanisms, not unlike those advocated by Anna Freud and the ego psychologists. Individuals repress
and deny aspects of their real selves that cannot be expressed under
the pressure of social life. Neurotics are not in touch with their feelings, and have to turn away from their real attitude to the world.
Rogers' theory proposes a split between the natural and the social;
an organismic process that is good and true, and a social world that
impedes and hinders. In this respect it is a formulation that directly
challenges that of Freud. Freud, it will be remembered, posited a
dangerous and destructive force that is civilised by society. For both

Freud and Rogers, neurosis is the price we pay for civilisation, but for Freud, it was a price worth paying.

We can see that Rogers' approach is a form of dualism that separates real inner selves from false outer expressions. Inner feelings are there to be discovered. This is a theory that is intensely individualistic. There is a clear split between the individual and the social world. It assumes an individual that precedes and is corrupted by the social world. Each person is a social atom, finding itself projected into a rather bleak and hostile social environment. People struggle to express their true natures, their idiosyncratic perceptions and meanings that they cannot expect to be understood by others. Here is Rogers:

> The only reality *I* can possibly know is the world as I perceive and experience it at the moment. The only reality you can possibly know is the world as *you* perceive and experience it at the moment. And the only certainty is that those perceived realities are different. There are as many 'real worlds' as there are people! (Rogers, 1980: 102)

Each person is a Cartesian self within a body frantically signalling to others in the vain hope of communicating. It is like a game of charades, where you cannot help but be frustrated by the inability to make your meaning clear to others.

In texts on personality, Rogers' theory is often called 'phenomenological'. We will begin to look at phenomenology in some detail in Chapter 5, but here we must note what is and is not phenomenological about the person-centred approach. Rogers was concerned with the description of individual experience; with understanding people and not resorting to mechanistic causal explanations of 'behaviour'. But true phenomenology attempts to outflank both Cartesian dualism and that dualism that separates the individual from the social world. Rogers mentions an assortment of existentialist thinkers who appear to authorise and add weight to his analysis, for example Buber, Kierkegaard and Sartre. But he does not really build on their thoughts, but rather raids them for occasional backing for his own ideas. Holland (1977) claims that he uses an existentialist vocabulary without really appreciating it. Rogers' phenomenology ignores the person's status of a 'being-in-the-world'. While it stresses the first-person accounts and perspective of individuals, it does not appreciate the person's embeddedness in the social world. This is in contrast to George Kelly, who Holland says rejects the vocabulary, but ends up inventing his own homespun version of existentialism.

Kelly's personal construct theory

Like Rogers, George Kelly's personal construct theory (PCT) was a product of his clinical work. And like Rogers' theory, it appears to European eyes to be very much a North American theory of personality. The person is at the mercy neither of unconscious forces nor simple laws of conditioning. Instead, people are actively in control of their destinies. This individualism parallels the 'log cabin to White House' story of Abraham Lincoln, stressing individual potential and responsibility rather than the weight of social structure in keeping people 'in their place'. Working in the economically depressed dust bowl of Kansas, Kelly recognised only too well the devastation brought about by forces beyond the individual's control. But what he draws our attention to is the extraordinary range of ways in which people can cope with and even overcome terrible adversity (Kelly, 1969c). The humanistic optimism of both Kelly and Rogers is a far cry from the tragic world view inherent in European psychoanalysis.

But Kelly's theory is in other ways very different from that of Rogers. There is no reference to 'growth', no inner self and no actualising tendency. Instead of the model of the person as a plant whose natural growth may be stunted, Kelly offered us the model of the person as scientist. This is in stark contrast to behaviourism's model of the person as a white rat or pigeon. The person the psychologist studies is not an inert mass of stimulus–response bonds, but an initiator of action. Like the psychologists who study them, people are, in effect, scientists, with their own theories about themselves and others. It is these theories that lie behind their behaviour, and if we want to work out why people do as they do, then we must understand their theories. We can see here the phenomenological aspect of PCT. It focuses on the way things appear to people, and Kelly and contemporary construct theorists have developed a number of interesting ways of investigating people's frames of references (Fransella, 2003). Of course, it makes no sense to ask whether people *really* are like scientists, plants, rats or computers. The point is, how useful is it to think of people like this; does it help us to see people's endeavours as similar to forming hypotheses, running experiments and drawing conclusions? It is this outlook of Kelly's, emphasising an 'as-if' way of approaching the world, that gives his theory the strong philosophical base so often lacking in personality theories. This philosophy is firmly grounded in American pragmatism.

Kelly (1955) wrote that the philosophy and psychology of John Dewey could clearly be read between the lines of the psychology of personal constructs. Dewey was one of the principal advocates of pragmatism (Thayer, 1982). This was a North American philosophical movement that was later eclipsed by the logical positivism that was the basis of behaviourism. Pragmatism emphasised the forward-looking nature of humankind and people's ability to intervene in nature to change the world to their advantage. Dewey saw the scientist as a moral hero, underlining how a critical scientific attitude had freed people from the crippling dogma of religion. The scientist tore up the rule book, asked heretical questions and dared to think differently. We can certainly see this spirit of Dewey in the writings of Kelly. The social psychology of Mead (see Chapter 5), who was a strong influence on Dewey, is also clearly visible. Kelly argued that scientific advance is not brought about by 'accumulative fragmentalism': the collecting of 'nuggets of truth' that are later assembled into a theory. If we look at the literature of trait theory, we can see thousands of publications about the trait profiles of people in different professions or psychiatric diagnostic categories. But these don't really advance our knowledge in any significant way. We can catalogue all these findings, but they don't really hang together and give us a bigger picture of personality. This is a 'bottom-up' approach to scientific advance that ignores the 'top-down' influence of new theory; the importance of a new searchlight that will enable us to pick out new patterns and develop a true understanding. This taking up of a new integrative perspective Kelly called 'constructive alternativism', and he declared it to be the philosophical basis of PCT. The proposition that people are scientists is a good example of constructive alternativism. The value of this claim is not to evaluated against some external reality (are people *really* scientists?), but in terms of its usefulness. So does it help to think of people as if they were scientists working in the light of their idiosyncratic theories? Kelly argued that when we are looking at people in trouble seeking psychological help, it is indeed a useful model of the person. So the reason why Kevin is shy might not be due to a lack of social skills. It might be that when we look at social life as it appears to Kevin, we notice that he thinks people are either sensitive or loudmouthed. Furthermore, he sees himself as very sensitive and hates 'loudmouths'. What we see as social competence, Kevin sees as loud and brash. It is therefore not surprising that he doesn't adopt what we see as socially skilled behaviour.

So for personal construct theorists personality is not represented by the traits people possess or the behaviours and internal dialogues they have learned. Neither is it caused by unconscious forces welling up from deep inside them. It is best conceived of in the ways that they see and make sense of things, or their construing. Personality is in the individual's perception and construction. Kelly proposed that the way people make sense of things and anticipate the future is through the use of a system of personal constructs that each person evolves in the light of her experience. He conceived of constructs as bipolar cognitive entities through which people make sense of what is happening. So constructs are like questions that we silently ask and which determine the sort of information we can make sense of (Burr and Butt, 1992). When John meets a new person, the most pressing issue for him might be whether he can impress this person, or if she is going to dominate him. Seeing the new person through the template of this construct may blind him to other things about her, for example whether she is nervous, looking for friendship or what she's interested in. The questions we ask determine the sorts of answer we can get. The reality that each of us encounters is thus filtered through personal construing.

We can see what looks at first glance like a similarity with Rogers. In the quote from Rogers above, he claimed that there were as many realities as there are people ('the only certainty is that those perceived realities are different'). But this similarity is only apparent. Kelly emphasised the idiosyncratic nature of construing because it was a useful clinical rule of thumb. PCT's main focus is in psychotherapy, and Kelly's principal aim was to produce a theory to guide clinical practice. The biggest mistake a clinical psychologist can make is to think 'here's another schizophrenic', or 'she's anorexic, I know what causes that'. It is best to assume that everyone is different, so that you are open to the personal meanings that guide this particular person's actions. But people are in many ways more alike than different. Kelly acknowledged that, within a culture, people often call on similar constructs to make sense of the world. In western societies, this is shown nicely by the way that we dip into the culturally common trait theory in order to anticipate other people. As I pointed out in Chapter 2, many of us think of others in terms of introvert–extravert and anxious–calm. But, as Mischel (1968) argued, this does not mean that people really have stable traits; the traits could be in the eyes of the beholders – representing their constructs. People find it useful to construe in trait terms because it helps to anticipate people and establishes a common vocabulary through which we can communicate with others. Kelly did not like what he saw as Rogers' phenomenology because it left individuals isolated in their own private worlds (Kelly, 1969d).

Although individuals may well use common constructs, what is idiosyncratic about each of us is that we each organise them into a personal system. So two people may both think in terms of what is fashionable and unfashionable. But they may disagree about what counts as fashionable. Kate may see fashion mainly in terms of the clothes people wear and the things they do in their spare time. For Richard it may centre on the ideas they have and what sort of car they drive. Here, fashionable–unfashionable is what Kelly called a 'superordinate construct' with respect to constructs relating to the evidence for it. Constructs such as well dressed–badly dressed are subordinate constructs. What a construct actually means is defined in terms of its implications within a particular person's construct system. Kate says she wants to be fashionable and Richard says he despises fashionable people, but they mean largely different things by this.

These systems evolve as a result of each person's experience. But it is important to note that this is not the same as saying what happens to them. A person's experience refers to the interpretation they place on the events that occur, not to the events themselves. Bill's comment might be read as insulting and abusive by me, whereas you see it as a rather clumsy but well-meaning joke. Our respective construing of Bill, as well as of people like him (whatever that means to us), then evolves in different directions, as we learn quite different lessons from the same event. From our experience we develop strategies that are designed to help us deal with things. So I might become extra sensitive to insults from people like Bill, and decide either to avoid them or get my retaliation in first. As a result, people like Bill will probably see me as having the trait of aggressiveness, but according to PCT, an appreciation of my personality depends on an understanding of my construing. And particularly important here is my construing of other people – how I act in the light of my construing of their constructions. This is where once again Kelly demonstrated his allegiance to pragmatism, this time by adopting George Mead's notion of sociality (Mead, 1982b). Kelly thought that conducting ourselves in a moral way necessitated construing other's intentions.

Only psychopaths treated others as objects and thought in terms of what they could do to or for them (Kelly, 1969e).

We can see that a construct system is not just a disembodied and rational cognitive structure. We invest in our construct systems; they are our only way of making any sense of the world, and when they prove inadequate in sense-making, our world shakes. This, said Kelly, is what we call the 'experience of emotion'. What Saint Augustine said about time can also be said of emotions: 'each of us understands it, yet none can explain it to another'. When you look at a psychology textbook, and turn to the chapter on emotions, you suddenly find yourself immersed in physiology and brain chemistry. As I argued in Chapter 2, there must be events taking place in the brain, but they do not explain human experience. Kelly tried to explain emotions with reference to construct systems, and I will illustrate this with reference to the experience of threat. Once again, Kelly's formulation grew out of his psychotherapeutic practice. Like the psychoanalysts before him, he noticed that, strangely, people frequently resist the change they think they want in therapy. He recognised that this was unconscious, in the sense that the construing behind it is preverbal and goes on beneath the level of awareness. In other words, people do not deliberate on their resistance, but find themselves resisting change. Change is threatening, and is explained by the awareness of immanent change in core structure. Core structure comprises the superordinate constructs about oneself; it can be thought of as a person's self-theory. So Kevin thinks of himself as sensitive rather than loudmouthed, friendly rather than confrontational. In the example I have used previously, his resistance to social skills training could be due to the threat of change. He would like to be less shy and more able to conduct himself confidently in public. But the way his construct system is arranged is problematic. Initiating contact and talking more both feel just too pushy to him, as he becomes in his eyes like the 'loudmouths' he despises. Thus psychological change for Kelly was more than behaviour change, and involves change in a person's construct system.

When we consider existential phenomenology in Chapter 5, we will see more clearly what Holland (1977) meant when he called Kelly a 'reluctant existentialist'. Kelly declared he was no existentialist, and distanced himself from phenomenology. These were labels he probably associated with Rogers, who shored up his theory with reference to a few European philosophers. Yet Kelly was inspired by the pragmatists whose philosophy shares many features with existential phenomenology. His theory is anti-reductionist, non-dualist and he refused to follow orthodox psychology in dividing people's experience into cognitive, affective and behavioural faculties. 'Construing' was a term that covered thinking, feeling and acting. Some contemporary construct theorists (Chiari and Nuzzo, 1996; Butt, 2003) have underlined this aspect of Kelly's work. Yet it is still seen both within and outside the constructivist community as essentially a cognitive theory. Constructs have come to be seen as personal cognitions (Ashworth, 2000), situated somewhere inside people and causing behaviour. It is easy to see Kelly as prefiguring the cognitive revolution in psychology. We have already noted that personality texts regard the work on cognitive schema as developing a parallel Kellian position. With the increasing dominance of the cognitive paradigm in psychology in the Anglophonic world, it is likely that it will be a cognitive reading of PCT that will be picked out by personality theorists. And Kelly himself gave plenty of support to this reading in his 1955 work. There he talked of constructs as being like things, cognitive entities. Yet in the collection of his essays edited after his death (Maher, 1969), this mechanistic feel is absent. Construing is something people do, rather than constructs being things they have. In my view, of all the theories that I have reviewed here, it is this non-cognitive reading of Kelly that offers the most fruitful understanding of people, and I will draw on it further in Chapter 5.

The person in psychoanalysis and humanism

All the approaches discussed in this chapter can be read as trying to understand people rather than explaining their behaviour in causal terms. They are not interested in drawing on psychological laws to change behaviour, but in helping people to stand back and make choices in their lives. Craib (2002: 16), sums this up when, writing from a psychoanalytic perspective, he comments: 'Increasingly, I see the value of my work as a psychotherapist not in terms of curing something, but in terms of understanding something.' This understanding, however, takes place in the context of (different) assumptions about human nature. From these strong and sometimes dogmatic assertions about human nature, therapists of different schools can always pick out evidence to support their theories. The psychoanalyst knows what she will find in unconscious material: evidence of envy, hatred and greed. The Rogerian will see evidence of the individual's thwarted growth and consequent defence mechanisms operating.

Construct theorists are most agnostic about the nature of the person but, even so, expect to find a structure of construing that is essentially bipolar. These clinically based theories have clearly all proved useful for some people. But the focus on therapy inevitably means that the role of the social world in understanding personality is underplayed. Although psychoanalytic and humanistic therapies pay a great deal of attention to the therapeutic relationship, the social interaction that they are focused on is reduced to the therapist–patient and mother–child dyads. There is always a concentration on what is going on 'inside' the person, whether this is conceived of as internalised object relations, feelings that the person is not in touch with, or personal constructs. The transference relationship in psychoanalysis points the way to an inner world, the good Rogerian allows the person to actualise and the construct therapist works towards challenging and elaborating the personal construct system. All too often, it is Ryle's ghost that is the subject of therapeutic operations.

What can be missed in all this is a proper social dimension to understanding people. The cultural is mistaken for the natural, as the psychological individual is taken as 'real', while society remains 'out there' and something of an abstraction. Occasionally, psycho-analysts make themselves look rather foolish when they stray out of their sociological depth and try to explain sociological phenomena in psychoanalytic terms. Fairbairn (1952) seemed to think that com-munism represented some sort of collective pathology (his own son became a Conservative MP), while others seemed to have had no doubt that homosexuality was a perversion. But most psychoanalysts never make such mistakes. For them, ORT is something that has application in the therapy room. Kelly (1955) distinguished between the focus and range of convenience of a theory. Its focus is the events that it is trying to explain and its range refers to its value outside this focus:

> The focus of convenience that we have chosen for our own theory-building efforts is the psychological reconstruction of life. We are con-cerned with finding better ways to help a person re-construe his life so that he need not be the victim of his past. If the theory we construct works well within this limited range of convenience, we shall consider our efforts successful and we shall not be too much disturbed if it proves to be less useful elsewhere. (Kelly, 1955: 23)

So perhaps what we think of as personality is a useful fiction, a good guiding myth for the purpose of psychotherapy? Perhaps if we want to understand people in their everyday lives, we have to look to a more social psychology? In the last two decades, social psychology in the English-speaking world has provided a strong critique of the concept of personality. It is to this critique that we will turn in Chapter 4.

4

The Social Constructionist Critique of Personality

In order to understand people, it has traditionally been assumed by psychologists that we have to look 'inside' them to find out what it is that is going on in their minds that causes their behaviour. The study of personality has been that part of psychology devoted to this pursuit. Of course, modern psychology does not talk about minds, but cognitive structures, construct systems and unconscious forces. But there remains an inside–outside distinction that is predicated on the assumption of the person as a psychological individual: one who is ultimately responsible for his actions. Nevertheless, it has always been recognised that situational context is important in producing behaviour, a point underlined by Mischel's (1968) work. As we have seen, those personality theories that have dealt with this do so by concentrating on how individuals construe and interpret their situations. They search for personal constructs or cognitive schema that account for personal meanings. This produces an interface with social psychology. Aronson et al. (2002: 12) see social psychology as located between 'its two closest intellectual cousins, sociology and personality psychology'. Modern social science maintains the distinction between the individual and society. Whereas sociology is said to be the study of society, social psychologists claim that their discipline is at the interface between psychology and sociology. It studies the individual's construing of the social world. This definition of social psychology reproduces the individualism we find in personality theory. Each individual is essentially a cognitive entity in his own skin, looking out at the world and trying to make sense of it. These social atoms then come together to take part in and fashion social life. This is what is meant when it is said that the individual precedes society.

However, in the last two decades of the twentieth century, a different type of social psychology emerged in the USA and the UK. This challenged the individualistic assumptions of orthodox social psychology, and built on a more sociological base to argue that individuals are the products of society rather than its creators. I will refer to this type of anti-individualistic approach as 'social constructionist', but since this is a field that is rapidly developing and indeed dividing, it is important to comment briefly on the sometimes confusing terminology associated with it. To North American psychologists, social constructionism refers almost exclusively to the work of Kenneth Gergen (1985, 1999). However, it is in the UK that this work has been most enthusiastically received and elaborated. British psychologists use the term far more loosely, using it to refer to a family of approaches (Burr, 1995). In the UK, the discursive psychologists (Harré and Gillett, 1994; Potter and Wetherell, 1995) as well as those calling themselves 'critical social psychologists' (Gaugh and McFadden, 2001) can be thought of as 'social constructionists'. Shotter (1993, 1995) labels his brand of constructionism 'dialogical psychology', and the term 'postmodern' has been applied to variants of constructionism (Kvale, 1992). I will focus mainly on what these approaches have in common, rather than on what divides them. Then I will consider how this approach might add a social dimension to our understanding of people. This will involve a critical examination of the roots of social constructionism in the work of Berger and Luckmann (1967).

Social constructionism

Having decided to adopt a broad rather than a narrow definition of social constructionism, we must now look at the core features of this family. Different commentators and critics define these in different ways. I will focus on what I see as some interrelated features: a critique of the modernist thought that underwrites traditional psychological approaches, leading to a perspective on the individual that sees it as a social product, one that is particularly formed by surrounding discourses.

Critique of modernist thought

I have already alluded to the concept of modernist science, indicating how the study of personality fits nicely into it. The modern era of science, with its search for laws governing the natural world, divided the field into various disciplines, one of which was psychology. Gergen (1992) claims that there were four overarching presumptions in modern psychology: the existence of a basic subject matter; the ultimate discovery of universal properties; an emphasis on experimental method; and a belief in research as progressive. Each of these is challenged in social constructionism, which depends on postmodern thought. The term 'postmodern' refers to a contemporary current of thought that some commentators see as a break with the modernist tradition. Other social scientists, for example Giddens (1991), recognise this trend, but prefer to see it as a continuation of modern thought. They therefore refer to it as 'late modern' thought.

A basic subject matter

As we saw when we considered the work of Ryle (1949), psychology was the science that assumed the role of studying the mind. Other sciences had their own preserves; biology had the body and sociology studied society. Psychological textbooks further subdivide their field, looking at various cognitive entities: attitude, motivation, emotion and personality. As I have already pointed out, these divisions set up puzzles concerning the interaction between mind and body as well as about how individuals influence (or are influenced by) society. Within psychology, questions arise about whether thoughts cause behaviour or how emotion affects thought. Social constructionism attempts to bypass these sorts of pseudo-puzzle by rethinking the individual–society relationship.

Universal properties

Modern psychology sought universal laws and principles that would allow us to produce beneficial personal change. But so many of these laws are in fact subject to local cultural factors. We saw in Chapter 2 that when it is claimed there is evidence of a dominant cognitive paradigm operating in the field of personality, the evidence came from publications in North American journals. As Gergen (1992) points out, this sort of finding is blind to the individualist ideology in which it is located. We would expect to find an emphasis on

individual cognition in a culture that prizes individual responsibility and effort; one which sees individuals' destinies largely in their
own hands. Social constructionism attempts to deconstruct the discourses in which our taken-for-granted assumptions are reproduced.
Its aim here is to stand back and to make figure out of the ground of
social context. Since observers can never entirely free themselves
from their cultural baggage, in the end all knowledge is perspectival
rather than value-free. For this reason, a cultural awareness and
reflexivity on the part of the researcher is essential.

Experimental method
Modern science wanted to predict and control the natural world. Its
success (as well as some of the costs) can be seen all around us. The
hope is that the searchlight of knowledge can be shone into the dark
corners of ignorance. When the aim of science is the discovery of universal laws, it follows that there has to be a very clear split between
the objective and the subjective. In experimental methods, researchers separate results (objective) from discussion (subjective interpretation). This Newtonian model has wide (although not universal)
application in the natural sciences. In an effort to follow the natural
sciences, modern psychology has often restricted its inquiry to those
areas that can be experimentally investigated. Qualitative and
idiographic methods were disregarded. Modern psychology's obses-
sion with the experimental method blinded it to the interpretive work
that is necessary in making sense of personal and social worlds. Social
constructionism uses methods adopted in other social sciences such as
interviews and discourse analyses in order to investigate the construction of realities. Here reflexive researchers offer their reading of
material, rather than claiming to have discovered universal truths.

Research as progressive
Modern science hoped that as more truths were revealed, it would
be able to build a bigger picture of the world, in which all these
pieces of the jigsaw fitted together. If only this were the case!
When we considered Kelly (1955), we noted that he called this vain
hope 'accumulative fragmenatalism'. Instead, knowledge advances
through paradigm shifts (Kelly's constructive alternativism). The
same pragmatism that underwrote PCT is drawn on in postmodern
thought. This argues, as we saw above, that all knowledge is from a
particular perspective, and must be examined not for how it represents an external reality, but what can be done with it. When this is

acknowledged, we can ask who this 'knowledge' serves, and why some types of research are funded and others are not.

So social constructionism positions itself as a postmodern approach to the person. It takes a critical approach to our taken-for-granted assumptions, insisting that there is nothing 'necessarily so' about people. It does not accept the idea found in folk wisdom and mirrored in personality theory that there is an essence inside each person that can be revealed through psychological investigation. Instead, it contextualises psychology, setting it within a cultural and ideological framework that it tries to explicate. It claims that the individual is not a pre-given entity, but a product of the social world.

Individual as a construction

In our present-day context, it is difficult not to think of biological individuals also as psychological individuals. Each person's skin seems to contain within it an individual mind with its particular wishes, worries and desires. But we must not mistake what seems natural for what might very well be a social product. Each of us is born into a society that predates us and we quickly take the constructed reality around us as natural. This internalisation is at the heart of Berger and Luckmann's thesis (1967) on which social constructionism is built and which we will examine in some detail later. While orthodox psychology's social psychology uncritically accepts the existence of a psychological individual, what sociology sees as social psychology is built on very different assumptions. This is sometimes called 'interpretive sociology' and argues that individuals are social constructions. This does not deny our experience of individuality, but points out that people are very different in different social contexts. So all 'constructed' means here is that things could have been put together differently. There is nothing pre-given and natural about our way of seeing things; different sorts of individual will be produced in different societies. It is, after all, difficult to think our way into the values of people in different cultures. The Japanese suicide pilots of World War II seemed just crazy to British and North American soldiers at the time. But these pilots had been brought up in a very different society, in which the samurai's Bushido code of conduct of self-discipline, courage and loyalty was venerated. Harré (1989) gives us a nice simile here. Each individual is like a fenced off piece of farmland. Farmers will develop their land differently from each other, and to each of them, their farm will look very different indeed from that of their neighbours. Yet each is subject to the same climate and similar soil. Consequently, the hill farms of the Yorkshire Dales are all much more alike than they are different. Unlike the farms of southern England, they rear sheep and do not grow wheat. Individual people are similarly forged out of local social conditions.

For the psychotherapist, it is important to focus on what is idiosyncratic about each person. But this should not blind us to what they have in common. And if we want to understand what makes people the way they are, we must appreciate the impact of the social world. After all, we cannot rely on psychotherapy to change everyone. If we want to produce more caring and empathic individuals, we must modify the climate and the soil in which people grow. This is why we have laws about child abuse and welfare. It is why we subscribe to beliefs about human rights.

Social constructionists back up their claim about the construction of the individual with reference to the writings of Foucault. He was a strong critic of modern thought and his work offers a bleak analysis of it. It often takes the form of something like: 'So you think liberal and progressive thinking is an advance on what happened before? Well think again!' His critique of penal reform in France is a good example of this (Foucault, 1977). His book opens with a horrific account of the public torturing to death of a would-be regicide in the eighteenth century. We recoil at the detailed planning that went into the execution. Then Foucault cuts to a description of the regime in a post-revolutionary prison, one hundred years later. No flogging, branding or public execution, just mind-numbing routine and discipline. (However, up until the 1860s, branding, flogging and public execution were still practised in England, giving Foucault's analysis a very local flavour.) What reason can there have been for this sudden change? A time traveller from ancient Rome would have recognised the eighteenth-century spectacle, but someone from 1750 would never have predicted the changes that took place in France by 1850. So what had happened? Foucault's answer was that sovereign power had been replaced by disciplinary power. The former relies on the sovereign's power to demonstrate publicly his authority on the body of the criminal. Disciplinary control works in a more subtle way, by attempting to get at the minds of criminals and 'reforming' them. Through regimes of discipline and by ensuring that criminals know that they might always be under surveillance, an attempt is made to get people to watch and hence control themselves. More humane it may be (and surely is), but Foucault claimed that the intention behind this 'advance' is its increased effectiveness in modern, complex societies. If you can get people to watch and regulate themselves, this is ultimately a far more effective method of social control.

Although we see disciplinary control par excellence in the prison, Foucault demonstrated its wider application in society. In the modern world, people are encouraged to watch themselves, compare themselves to others and find themselves wanting. The reflective individual internalises the watchful eye and the critical voice of a disapproving generalised other. Freud thought of the superego as a natural consequence of the oedipal period, mistaking this social product for a natural maturational process. But Foucault saw Freud's whole focus on sexuality as a typical example of misguided modern thought. The modernist story that is uncritically accepted is that in Victorian times, sexuality became repressed as innate desires went underground. More recently, this repression has been lifted and people are now freer to express themselves. Foucault's take on this is quite different (Foucault, 1981). He argued that sexuality in its modern form had, in effect, been talked into existence. Of course sodomy had always been practised, but in pre-modern times, there weren't types of people called homosexuals. With the advent of the Victorian sexologists (for example Havelock Ellis, Iwan Bloch and Richard von Kraft-Ebbing), sexual perversions were created that resembled mental illnesses. An extended vocabulary of pathology was invented that is still in use in contemporary psychiatry. Foucault saw modern societies as imposing their norms and values through the use of a discourse of the natural. Doctors declared people who did not conform as ill and perverted, and people then watched themselves for signs of pathology. Psychoanalysis was a secular form of the confessional in which the expression of desire was effectively controlled. In the Roman Catholic confessional, people confess their sins, do penance and are absolved by a priest who mediates between them and God. In psychoanalysis, the analyst stands between the person and the unconscious. Now neither God nor the unconscious may in fact exist, but there is no doubt that a belief in both serves to control those who believe in them. In these secular times it may be that psychology and psychoanalysis allow for more effective control than does the concept of God. Foucault claimed that the elaborated discourse on sexuality did not really liberate people, but instead enmeshed them further in the net of power. We look at ourselves, compare ourselves to some mythical ideal and worry that we are perverted. The self-surveillance of disciplinary control does authority's job most effectively.

So, for Foucault and those constructionists that follow him, the individual as we know it today is a necessary social product of complex modern societies. The reflective self-process that we have in modern times is the result of an increasing and pervasive regulative force. This bleak analysis forms the basis for the emphasis on power in social constructionism. In many ways, Foucault's argument is not very different from that of the labelling theorists (Scheff, 1966). But labelling theory came out of symbolic interactionism (of which more later) and did not have the stress on malevolent power structures in society.

A focus on language

In the section above I referred to the 'discourse of the natural'. Social constructionists focus strongly on the role of language in the construction of a shared social reality and conduct discourse analyses (Willig, 1999) to demonstrate this. There is no simple definition of discourse, because two different philosophical traditions are drawn on to deal with language usage: the Continental philosophy of Foucault and the British analytic philosophy of Wittgenstein and Austin. There is certainly a difference in emphasis as well as flavour in these two. Nevertheless, I will concentrate on what they have in common; the power of language to shape and guide our thinking and action. Of course language is itself such a very good example of a social construction. No individual or committee of individuals created the English language, yet it is real enough, facilitating and hindering our expression. We have an extended vocabulary of feeling and emotion (what Foucault claimed was the product of modern thinking) that is not always easily translated into other languages. And the fine discriminations in other languages (for example the naming of different types of snow for the Inuit) are not available in English.

The discursive psychologists – Harré (1989) and Potter and Wetherell (1987) – as well as Shotter (1993) draw on the philosophy of the later Wittgenstein (1972). He argued that the meaning of words cannot be made clear by dictionary definitions, that is, with reference to other words. This is rather like explaining what money is by translating euros into dollars. We can only appreciate the meaning of money by seeing how it is used. Seeing how people buy and sell with money makes sense of it. Only then can we understand why people would steal or work for it. Knowing how words are used tells us of their meaning, and for this, we have to see how they are embedded in different 'language games', the rule-governed ways that words are used. So we use words to express ourselves in different language games. Promising, warning, naming and describing are all examples of such games. Behaviourist psychologists made the mistake of thinking that all language was to do with description. An adult says 'cat' to a baby pointing at a cat and the baby associates the sound and later the spelling with the small furry animal – 'cat' now signals cats correctly. But most of our language is more complicated than this. We do things with it – persuading, warning and cajoling. When, for example, we name someone or something – perhaps a baby, a ship or indeed a cat – we are not describing it. And language games only make sense when they in their turn are embedded in what Wittgenstein called 'forms of life', shared sets of cultural assumptions that have developed in different societies. Recently, I was at King's Cross station in London and saw the words *Archbishop Thomas Cranmer* on a railway engine. Just what would someone from China or India have made of this? Perhaps he might mistake it for an advert or a charm? In the UK we know it is the engine's name only because we have the rather peculiar practice of naming railway engines. We see here that hermeneutic understanding that works through the contextualising which I outlined in Chapter 1 when I used 'turning up' as an example.

Now, as I said, historically, psychologists have been somewhat naive about language, recognising language only as descriptors. Consequently, when trying to understand people, we might think that they are struggling to describe inner feelings. Liz might say she is hurt by some comment you made yesterday and consequently is feeling particularly sensitive today. The dualism that pervades personality theory (and both reflects and is reflected in popular psychology) leads us to think that she is reading some internal meter and reporting on it. But this cannot be what is going on, Wittgenstein claimed. Each individual cannot possess a private language and inner set of meanings that he tries to communicate to others. Language is a social construction. Skinner (1974) made a very similar point. We learn to use descriptions correctly because the verbal community can see our mistakes and help us to discriminate properly. When a child labels something orange rather than yellow, we can see that a mistake has been made and shape language use accordingly. But the verbal community has no access to private events. How can you possibly know that I am using terms like 'sensitive' and 'hurt' in the way that you would? So when Liz says she is hurt and feeling sensitive, this cannot be interpreted correctly as a description. But perhaps it is a warning. She might in effect be saying 'don't push your luck today!' This is what Harré (1989) means when he says that so many psychological problems are really grammatical problems. Interpreting what is meant is a matter of understanding language use, that is, what language games are in play.

Foucault's work does not contradict this analysis, but adds a dimension of power to any discourse analysis. Discursive psychologists tend to focus on local micro-interactions, looking at how people draw on interpretive repertoires to do something. But Foucault situates such interactions in a broader context. He concentrated mainly on the language game of the confessional, and how this ensnares the individual in a surrounding web of power. In the confessional, the individual searches for inner imperfections, declares sins and is thereby absolved from them. Up until the seventeenth century, Foucault (1981) tells us, the practice had been restricted to the clergy. But it was extended to the general population during the Counter-Reformation. This sought to tie individuals to the Catholic Church in the face of the threat from the new Protestantism. Psychology, psychiatry, psychotherapy and psychoanalysis (sometimes referred to as the 'psy-complex') all provide a secular version of the confessional through which individuals were brought under the control not of the church, but of the state. They reproduced the Judeo-Christian message that the flesh was the source of all evil, encouraging people to tell everything in order to free themselves. Sex was converted into discourse as secret desires were examined and pondered. Individuals do not find themselves in this self-scrutiny; instead they create themselves. It is within a discursive space that individuals chart their notions of self and identity.

The person in social constructionism

So we can see that an understanding of people from a social constructionist perspective is very different from that of personality theory. Instead of looking inside people, looking for causal mechanisms in brain structure, cognitive entities or unconscious forces, the constructionist looks to the discourses that constitute the person. Of course each individual is a mass of neurones and biological predispositions.

But these bodies can be shaped into virtually anything by the social forces that work on them. If we could take the same biological machinery and set it in ancient Rome rather than twenty-first century London, we would see an entirely different individual being formed. Without the contemporary discourses of human rights and equal opportunities, along with the climate of possessive individualism in which these discourses have flourished, we might find that any of us would enjoy an afternoon at the games, watching an orgy of rape, torture and butchery. To understand people is to see them in a social and historical context. Of course there will be differences between individuals, but the similarities outweigh these differences. If time travellers from a thousand years ago were to be parachuted into a university campus today, what would they see? Not the fine differences in clothing and fashion that we might pick up. They would see us as all the same and different from them. This is because we are blind to social forces that operate on us all, whereas these would be obvious to someone who did not share this context. While personality theories point out the differences between us, social constructionism reminds us that we are all fashioned out of the same material. Psychologists need reminding of this, even though it is obvious to other social scientists, historians, anthropologists and sociologists. To these groups, social constructionism is nothing new, just social psychology's belated acknowledgement of a social world.

Yet there is a paradox in this sudden conversion: there is very little room at all for personal agency in this new social psychology. Social constructionism is avowedly anti-humanistic. The paradox is that the social sciences, with their roots in the social world, allow for a greater degree of personal construction and agency. In both history and sociology, there is an attempt to come to terms with personal agency when it is placed in the context of social structure. We all feel as though we are free agents choosing to act as we do, but it is clear that social structures (like language) limit what we can do and even think about. Marx famously said that people make history, but not in circumstances of their own choosing. In sociology, this agency/ structure debate is a problem that has been wrestled with in all its complexity (Walsh, 1998). But social constructionism represents a pendulum swing in psychology from agentic to structural explanation. This reflects the adoption of a particularly anti-humanistic strand of French thought and it is particularly prominent in critical social psychology. This is associated with Althusser, Lacan and Foucault and the labels 'structuralism' and 'poststructuralism' are sometimes used to describe it. I am not even going to try to define these terms because they are hotly contested on the basis of very fine differences. For our purposes, it will be enough to note that the person is reduced to one who merely holds a subject position in either an ideological or a discursive field. This is why in this tradition they talk of the subject rather than the person. And this is not the subject as used in 'subjective', with its phenomenological connotations. It is subject in the sense that one is the subject of a sovereign. In this case, people are subject to either an ideology being force-fed them, or a discourse that positions them. People are passive and moved around by forces beyond their control. The replacement of sovereign with disciplinary power simply changes the forces to which the individual is subject. Here it is economic forces that ultimately pull the puppet-person's strings, through the medium of political ideology and discourses.

Discursive psychology does not have the strong political flavour of so-called 'critical psychology'. Burkitt (1999) calls both Gergen's constructionism and discursive psychology varieties of 'light' social constructionism. These focus on a micro-level of interaction; the ways in which people conduct their day-to-day interactions and discursive practices. He distinguishes light constructionism from Foucault's 'dark' type, which emphasises the influence of power at a more macro-level. For discursive psychology, the ultimate reality is the person in conversation. Our sense of self arises in interaction with others, and is due to the sum of the discursive positions that we take up. I have already mentioned that, following Wittgenstein, Harré (1989) argues that many psychological puzzles are due to grammatical confusion. Because we are used to using the pronoun 'I' so frequently, we come to think of it as an internal cognitive entity, whereas it really only denotes a subject position in discursive space. When we ask someone why he did something, it sounds at first as though he is giving us an account of causality. So, Anne might say she lost her temper because she was tired of Ken's excuses for always being late. But really, she hasn't told us what caused her to lose her temper and shout at Ken. She has given us her reason and why it was justifiable. She has told us why it was reasonable to act as she did, and backed this up by contextualising her action. Harré points out that first-person accounts always have this quality; they are moral justifications and not causal statements. Discursive psychology's discourse analysis (Potter and Wetherell, 1987) aims to tease out the complex ways we use discourse to position ourselves like this. It is commendably anti-dualist. But as Ashworth (2000) comments, if we are interested in fully understanding people, it surely stops too early. It shows *how* people do indeed draw on discursive resources available to them, but does not address the question of *why*. It ignores individuals' struggle to convey something of their life-worlds to others. It is concerned solely with what people do with their talk and the resources they draw on to do it.

For both Gergen (1999) and Shotter (1993) the focus of constructionism is the person in relation. Gergen stresses how, in our postmodern times, people have a far wider range of relationships than in even the recent past. It is increasingly difficult to hold on to the myth of a single true self for each of us when we find ourselves distributed across so many different interactions – at home, work, with friends, partner, clubs and on the internet. Rather like Mischel's (1968) emphasis on the situation-specificity of behaviour, our increasing variety of interactions and conversations highlights the contextual nature of the self. Shotter (1993) builds on the symbolic interactionist concept of 'joint action' to make a similar point. I will have a lot more to say about this idea in Chapter 5, but briefly, it refers to the way in which we find our action drawn out of us in the presence of others. It is so often the case that what goes on between people is more important than what goes on in the minds of any individual participant when we are trying to trace who did what.

So, in social constructionism, the self emerges through interaction and conversation. There is no core, no central essence to the person. What we may think of as the light types focus on local interactions and conversations as the ground on which the individual is built. Harré (1989) argued that to have a self means in fact to have a self-theory; one that the person refers to and uses to assess his own actions. The discourse analysis that is the basis for research is not interested in a world beyond the text or language. In this sense it seems to stop well short of Wittgenstein's intention to ground language in its use and in forms of life. For 'dark' social constructionism, the self is the product of the ideology that accompanies modern thinking. Here there is a deep suspicion about every modern move and every aspect of individualism. There is even apparent a sentimentality about any collectivised or pre-modern society. When reading some critical psychologists' attacks on all forms of individualism, it is worth reminding oneself just how loathsome it would be to live in societies that either predated or rejected modernism – ancient Rome, seventeenth-century Europe, Hitler's

Germany or Stalin's Russia. While there is a disbelief in any form of rationality or agency, there is sometimes an extraordinary flirtation with the psychoanalytic unconscious. In an effort to explain individual desires that are difficult to account for in terms of subject positions, the impenetrable writing of the French psychoanalyst Lacan are sometimes recruited. But people are always subjects and in no sense citizens. They are subject to the pushes and pulls of social structure, ideology, discourses and perhaps the unconscious. They appear to have minimal control over their lives. To believe otherwise is to be a plaything of ideology and perhaps even a tool of oppression. Discourse analysis for dark constructionism is a way of revealing the subtle methods of oppression, the operation of disciplinary power through pervasive discourses.

Social constructionism certainly offers us a new social dimension to consider in the project of understanding people. Most personality theorists see the person's skin as separating an inside environment from an outside society and this dualism is properly challenged in social constructionism. But here the skin is an entirely permeable membrane, allowing social forces to determine action through the media of ideology and discourses. Personal agency is rejected and social determinism accepted. What is so strange and indeed disappointing about this is the restricted use of thought from sociology, where the agency/structure debate has been creatively addressed by several theorists (Berger and Luckmann, 1967; Giddens, 1984; Bordieu, 1998; Archer, 2000). In fact, in his article in which Gergen set out his ideas on social constructionism and launched it to a wide audience of North American psychologists (Gergen, 1985), there is an interesting footnote in which he pays tribute to the work of Berger and Luckmann (1967). This footnote is very frequently referred to in the social constructionist literature, but the ideas of Berger and Luckmann (1967) are never developed. In fact, many in the field even misspell Luckmann's name! But it is to Berger and Luckmann's *The Social Construction of Reality* that I now want to turn. This is because we can see in it the roots of the social constructionism that have not been properly elaborated.

The social construction of reality

Berger and Luckmann's book was an attempt to reconcile two competing paradigms in sociology. Forty years ago, the orthodox position in the discipline was one that saw social structure as a determining factor that ruled the lives of individuals born into a particular society. Society was a social fact, a reality with which individuals had to cope but could not escape. The social determinists point out that society is not an abstraction; it is all around us, gets inside us and constantly exercises its deterministic force. We fall into role positions that pre-exist us, unknowingly follow implicit rules and obey the normative imperatives that surround us. It is easy to appreciate the force of this view. Think of how we take on fashions – in clothes, activities and the naming of our children. Each of us thinks we are making free choices, but it is clear that we are internalising patterns and owning them. We can see here how dark social constructionism provides a good example of this view. On the other hand, there existed an agentic view, one that emphasised individual agency in creating society. The symbolic interactionists claimed that we do not just take on pre-existing roles, but actively interpret the actions of both others and ourselves. People can and do change society, make innovations and exert a degree of free choice. Both arguments are indeed compelling. But if we are trying to understand ourselves and others, it makes a great deal of difference whether we conceptualise people as free agents or mere puppets.

Berger and Luckmann's solution to the agency/structure problem was to insist that both positions were correct: people are both made by society and in their turn reproduce it. The social world in which we live appears to us as a social reality. It appears as real to us as does the natural world. It does not seem to be provisional and constructed. When you wander round a busy city centre, you maintain a demeanour that is in keeping with the situation. You don't touch others and they don't touch you. You get on a crowded train and avert eye contact, gazing seriously at the adverts or out of the window. When you meet someone who mutters to themselves, stands too close to you and glares at you, you might think they are mad. Social rules are not explicit, but we all know them, and we know when they are broken. The rules seem natural, not made up. But society is indeed a construction, one put together by other people, a construction to which each of us contributes. You can become aware of this if you visit a different country and discover that there are different rules in operation. It must have been people who created the rules and produced the different languages. But no one did it deliberately. There was never a committee that sat and considered how people should behave and how they shouldn't. To explain this paradox, Berger and Luckmann (1967) proposed a dialectical relationship between the individual and society. A dialectical relationship is one in which what goes on between the two parties in a relationship determines the development of each. So the individual and society are not two different types of substance, with one producing the other. The question is not, which controls which? Instead, both unfold in the light of the other and the two cannot be considered as isolated and separate entities.

Berger and Luckmann (1967) proposed that there were three moments in this particular dialectic: internalisation, externalisation and objectivation. All three are going on all the time, but in the life of any individual, the cycle begins with internalisation. Each of us is born into a social world that predates us and comes to have the character of a pre-given reality. Humankind is possessed of a uniquely plastic nature, capable of living in a vast range of environments. Unlike tortoises, tarantulas and koalas, we adapt to almost any climate and any situation. We therefore have an extended infancy and childhood and are not biologically determined, the creatures of instinct, in the way that other animals generally are. We internalise rules, norms and roles in the way that they are given to us and taken for granted. Berger and Luckmann (1967) draw on Mead's (1934) social psychology here. In primary socialisation, the infant learns to see himself through the eyes of significant and, later, generalised others, fashions a self and acts accordingly. In complex modern societies, this is elaborated in secondary socialisation, where different subgroups modify our social action. We might look back on our time at university and conclude that it was the time of greatest change in our lives. This will be because of the effect of the internalisation of a new social world, with its different rules and roles.

Each person then acts in the light of the way in which things appear to them. This is the second moment in the dialectic: externalisation. An individual's action is not determined by society, but is clearly facilitated and constrained by it. Everybody is capable of innovation (perhaps some more than others), but we all build on what is already there. The inventions of the twentieth century could not have been produced out of nowhere a hundred years ago. Computer technology has provided the ground on which so many innovations are built. One could not have conceived of the internet in even the recent past. As we saw when we looked at cognitive-behavioural approaches to personality, present conceptions of personality depend in no small degree on this technological advance. Of course, we may reject what is already there, but we do not just ignore it. When John Watson issued his behaviourist manifesto a century ago, he rejected the pragmatism of his PhD supervisor, George Mead. Contemporary psychology is still living with the consequences, as psychology became defined in many ways as 'not Mead', and Mead's work came to be seen as sociology.

Here we see that our externalisations often have a quality that transcends our immediate situation. A gesture, a spoken word or a glance come and go fleetingly. But many externalisations become objectivated in the third moment in Berger and Luckmann's dialectic. The things people do leave traces that speak of their social organisation. Humankind imbues everything with meaning. Objects for us always seem to contain something of a human presence. As I look around my desk, I see a pen that was my father's. For me it's always 'dad's pen', and whenever I pick it up or look at it, it has something of him in it. Presents are not just books, clocks or CDs. They are the books, clocks or CDs that a particular person gave us, and they seem to contain their love or affection. Society is made up of material objectivations. Since Victorian times, there has been a myth in England that the countryside is in some way natural. It was sentimentalised during the Industrial Revolution. Contrasting with the obvious filth and pollution of the cities, the countryside came to stand for everything that was good, clean, honest and truly English – the village green, the game of cricket and the warm beer. But very little in the English countryside is natural. It has been fashioned by several thousand years of rural society. The fields, the animals, the hedgerows – all have been carefully bred and cultivated to provide produce. When red telephone boxes appeared in the mid-twentieth century, they were abhorred as a scar on the countryside. When they disappeared some decades later, they were mourned. And it is not just in material artefacts that we see objectivation. Written language and the printed word lay down a sediment of thought that is there to be internalised by future generations. It is these objectivations that illustrate that there is nothing abstract about society. In the moment of internalisation, we take for granted the objectivations that everywhere surround us. Just a nature abhors a vacuum, humankind's plastic nature abhors a lack of social structure. We are social animals that require the framework that is provided by a cultural setting.

Berger and Luckmann (1967) saw the natural world not only as a buzzing booming confusion, but also a dangerous one. The social structure in which we are embedded lends us a sense of support.

Everyday rituals and conversation maintain this social reality. Nothing makes sense without a social context. Reviewing Berger's work, Abercrombie (1986: 24) cites an experiment in which a married couple were asked to write down an ordinary conversation that they had one morning. It became clear that the meaning of everything said was coded in such a way that anyone else would have difficulty in interpreting it. It depended on a set of prior assumptions that in their turn were grounded in further taken-for-granted assumptions that it was virtually impossible to spell out. So many of our interactions are like this. Just try explaining exactly what is funny about something you observe. The reason why sharing a sense of humour is seen as such an important thing between close friends is that it tells of a shared social world. So we jointly construct a social world that has the quality of the real about it. It simultaneously supports, facilitates and constrains us. Thus we are not individuals before we enter this world; instead we are the creations of it.

The roots of constructionism

However, the constructionism of Berger and Luckmann (1967) is substantially different from the social constructionism of contemporary social psychology. Its roots are in interpretive microsociology. This is a complementary mixture of existential phenomenology and symbolic interactionism. These approaches will be examined more fully in Chapter 5, because I will argue that they form the basis of a true understanding of people. Here, I want to show how Berger and Luckmann's work is rooted in these traditions. As sociologists, they recognised the force of society in the constitution of the individual. But they rejected any social determinism, stressing the agency of the person. The person is indeed socially constructed but, once constructed, is a centre for some degree of agency and choice. In the moment of externalisation, one reproduces the institutions objectivated in society. So, in contemporary western society, we make friends, just as have past generations. The concept is objectivated in the word, and we interpret and recognise our affection for another within its framework. Language provides an ever-present tool for the production of objectivations. But we also innovate and create new friendships and indeed new types of friend. Giddens (1992) notes how in the recent past the social ties of kinship have been weakened and people rely increasingly on the 'pure relationship', that bond with others based purely on affection and not on the reciprocal obligation of kinship. This has been enabled by various macrosocietal changes, but the point is that people are creative, they are not puppets dancing at the ends of the strings of social structure. Material changes in society create opportunities that people then use and reflect upon. This point was strongly established by Berger:

> Unlike puppets, we have the possibility of stopping our movements, looking up and perceiving the machinery by which we have been moved. In this act lies the first step towards freedom. And in this same act we find the conclusive justification of sociology as a humanistic discipline. (Berger, 1963: 176)

Thomas Luckmann was even more influenced by phenomenology than Berger, and *The Social Construction of Reality* begins with an examination of the way in which the social world appears to people. In their opening chapter, Berger and Luckmann (1967: 34) state that an appreciation of phenomenology must come before any sociological analysis. We must ask how it is that people come to take for granted the social world in the same way that they do the physical world. They note how everyday life presents itself to us as an intersubjective reality. This means that we take for granted that others experience the world as we do; it is not a dream. 'I know that my natural attitude to this world corresponds to the natural attitude of others, that they also comprehend the objectifications by which this world is ordered' (p. 37). In their phenomenological analysis, they also note how our connection to the world is ultimately pragmatic. The 'here' of my body and the 'now' of my present dictate my primary concern. As we will see in Chapter 5, this emphasis on the world as it appears to the particular embodied person is the hallmark of existential phenomenology. This was a tradition rejected by Foucault, and the structuralists who form the foundation of critical social psychology today. For them, individuals are carried along by the tide of discourse, however things may appear to each of them. A preliminary phenomenological analysis is therefore irrelevant to any understanding of people.

In Berger and Luckmann's view, people do not passively soak up ideologies and discourses. Instead they make some sort of sense of it through their interaction with others. This is where symbolic interactionism complements phenomenology, focusing on what Goffman (1983) termed the 'interaction order'. This is the everyday transactions between friends, lovers, club members, performers and audiences that are, for the symbolic interactionists, the foundations of society. (From a structuralist perspective, these interactions are merely the effects of structural forces.) Berger and Luckmann's socialisation relies heavily on the work of Mead (1934). Here, individuals don't just take up subject positions within a discursive field, but take up the perspectives of others. Through this process, individuals develop a sense of self and engage in internal dialogues that mediate their action. It is through this deliberation that there exists a personal agency, an ability to 'perceive the machinery by which we have been moved'.

So Berger and Luckmann's is a phenomenological and interactionist sociology. I think we can see how Gergen was influenced by it when we consider his phenomenological approach, standing back and looking again at the modern individual. But it is an approach that is largely absent in the British versions of social constructionism: discursive psychology and critical social psychology. Here, discourse analyses don't carry through the analysis to look at the person as discourse user, as an indicator of a life-world. People are subject to discourses, and the discourses are therefore the object of analysis. This social constructionism is a useful counterweight to the individualism of personality theory, but the person in it evaporates entirely. As Craib (1998) observes, social constructionism, based as it is on the turn to language, certainly has something to say about the understanding of people, but it does not have *everything* to say. It ignores the personal agency that was emphasised by both Mead (1934) and Berger and Luckmann (1967). I think that an opportunity for psychology has been missed in the way that social constructionism has developed in such an anti-humanistic way. In the next chapter, I will unpack the interpretive understanding that I have referred to above. This, I will argue, offers the most useful avenues to understanding ourselves.

PART II

An Existential Phenomenological
Approach

5

Interpretive Understanding

In this chapter, I want to draw together the elements of interpretive understanding that can help us to make sense of those aspects of ourselves and others that are the focus of personality theories. These will come from three related sources: hermeneutics, existential phenomenology (particularly the work of Merleau-Ponty) and the social psychology of Mead. Throughout I will try to show the linkage between these different frameworks. This will be done primarily with reference to Berger and Luckmann's *The Social Construction of Reality* (1967). Frequently cited as a 'seminal work' by social constructionists, we will see that the foundations of their constructionism are very different from the anti-humanism of both discursive psychology and critical social psychology. I will also make reference to Kelly's personal construct theory. This is because in many ways it elaborates important aspects of these frameworks in the area that we are interested in: personality.

The phrase 'interpretive understanding' has been used in the social sciences to refer to a tradition that originated in German thought in the nineteenth century. It has been translated from the German word *verstehen* and is associated with, among others, Dilthey, Simmell and Weber (see Outhwaite, 1975). This tradition comprises a complex mixture of the thought of these and other social philosophers, but it is neither possible nor necessary to trace the fine grain of these relationships here. However, it will be useful to say something about this tradition. Psychology is an extraordinarily ahistoric science, and this is perhaps one of the reasons why it appears to have reinvented the wheel of social constructionism without looking at and properly building upon the work of those who have gone before. Having noted some of the important features of *verstehen*, and in particular its relationship to hermeneutics, I will focus on phenomenology and Mead's social psychology, which together form the foundations of the work of Berger and Luckmann (1967).

Verstehen and hermeneutics

We have already noted how the Enlightenment in Europe led to a valorisation of science. The discovery of natural laws and the mastery of the environment had depended on the adoption of a scientific method that demanded a disinterested objective approach on the part of scientific investigators. These experimenters stood back from their work and distanced themselves from subjective interpretations in an effort to arrive at once-and-for-all truths about the world. Scientific explanation followed the rule of deductive logic. From theories and principles, testable hypotheses were derived and tested, preferably in controlled experiments. In this way, causal relationships were discovered as nature gave up its secrets to the relentless inquiry of humankind. It was assumed that the social sciences should follow a similar route in their quest to understand people either individually or in society. We can see that psychology, alone among the social sciences, still clings to this project. Psychology is primarily a laboratory-based enterprise, where laws governing behaviour are sought, later to be applied in various fields: clinical, educational and occupational (all this I alluded to in Chapter 1).

Those in the *verstehen* tradition, however, insisted that while this type of explanation was appropriate in the natural sciences, the social sciences called for a different type of understanding – *verstehen*. Social scientists, according to this view, should not try to provide causal explanations – prediction and control is not the aim in the social sciences. It is practically impossible to achieve the distance and disinterest of the natural scientist when the objects of study are other human beings. The psychologist and the sociologist are already immersed in the social world, sharing a perspective on things through common social practices like language. This is a commonality of outlook that cannot be discarded at will. Outhwaite (1975: 16–17) outlined the social sciences project:

> social phenomena, and in particular, human action, are not 'given to' the investigator in the same way as natural phenomena. The social scientist must begin with data which are already partially interpreted in the ordinary language of everyday life. Moreover, social scientists cannot coherently aim to provide a natural science of human life, but rather deepen,

systematise and often qualify by means of empirical and conceptual investigations, an understanding which is already present.

So any analysis inevitably builds upon and is from the perspective of immersion in a social world that predates and is a condition for it. An understanding of the human social world precedes and is the ground for further explanations of it. This was the position of Dilthey, who began to develop hermeneutics as a method in the social sciences. This line of argument was later elaborated by Heidegger and Gadamer (see Warnke, 1987).

Hermeneutics

Hermeneutics was originally a method used to interpret religious texts during the Reformation in Europe. Until the rise of Protestantism, the Catholic Church had insisted on religious meaning being mediated by priests. The use of awe-inspiring rituals and the Latin language ensured that God's work remained a mystery to everyday people. But the Protestants argued that the meaning of religious texts could be understood directly through a careful reading; what psychologists might today consider to be a form of discourse analysis. The argument in contemporary social psychology about whether any reading can tell us of the author's intentions began then. At the turn of the eighteenth century, Schleirmacher argued for both psychological and grammatical analyses. Each had its place, with the former focusing on the author while the latter rested with an analysis of the text itself. Dilthey recognised and elaborated this distinction (see Outhwaite, 1975). Clearly, sometimes a particular focus is appropriate and another is not. When we are confronted with any text, we approach it as though it is trying to say something to us. If we are reading a confession or a diary, it seems particularly important to try to understand the intention of the author. It is vital to know what is to be taken seriously, what is meant ironically and what she is trying to say about her life. Only then can we interpret the meaning in the text. But if we are trying to make sense of an academic article, the author fades into the background in comparison to what is being said. The content and style of presentation is all-important. Knowing facts about the author's state of mind are irrelevant to understanding. As I write this, the rain is pounding down outside my window and I have a slightly depressed feeling about it and the prospects for a walk later. None of this is necessary for you to appreciate as you read what I am saying about hermeneutics. However, it might be important if I was writing a different sort of text; if this was an autobiography, my characteristic moods might be a feature of central interest.

There is some dispute among hermeneutic scholars about the balance between these two functions in an analysis. Gadamer (1975) argued that we can never fully empathise with an author, and we delude ourselves if we consider it possible. So when we try to understand a historical text, we can never put ourselves in the author's position, because we have a historical perspective that was not available at the time of writing. This point is well-illustrated by the puzzle: if you found a Roman coin with '15BC' on it, how would you know it was a fake? Well, because Romans in 15BC could have no idea that hundreds of years later, the birth of Christ was to become a pivotal point in the calendar in the western world. Yet today we could not begin to think about the period without being conscious of this issue. Similarly, a historian listening to one of Churchill's parliamentary speeches made in 1940 could not really understand the meaning of the speech then, either to the author or those that heard it. This is because we now know the outcome of World War II and think of this period as Britain's darkest moment. People then, including Churchill, could not know that, soon, Hitler would invade Russia, and Japan would bring the USA into the war on Britain's side. Dilthey (see Rickman, 1997) recognised the problems of empathy, but advocated both aspects of a hermeneutic analysis. Here we see the issue that is now being played out in the disputes surrounding contemporary discourse analysis. With different emphases, both Gadamer and Derrida follow in Heidegger's anti-humanist footsteps, focusing exclusively on a textual analysis to the exclusion of authorial intention. We can pick out their heirs in both the dark and light forms of contemporary social constructionism.

The interpretation of texts

However, it is Dilthey's work (1988) that I am interested in here. It is his notion of understanding, and the *verstehen* tradition generally, that is the progenitor of the interpretive understanding evident in both phenomenology and symbolic interactionism. Dilthey's focus was on the interpretation of historical texts, but as we shall see, phenomenology has extended the range of convenience of his approach to a consideration of a general understanding of people. For Dilthey there was no Archimedian fixed point from which knowledge of the world can be deduced. In this he contrasts sharply with both Descartes, who wanted to start with disembodied consciousness, and the empiricists for whom the objective world becomes known through our senses. Dilthey argued that understanding can only be achieved through a hermeneutic circle; a to-and-fro movement between the whole text and the parts that constitute it. So we can only understand words by looking at how they are used in a sentence and we can only understand a sentence with reference to the words that make it up. 'She's got a brand-new car' and 'She's wearing a new brand of jeans' are sentences in which the meaning of 'brand' is quite different, yet we have no difficulty in understanding either meaning and do not confuse the two. Without deliberate thought, we achieve understanding by examining both words and the context in which they are situated. In a similar way, we might think of people as texts to be read and understood in terms of the hermeneutic circle. Outhwaite (1975) points out that when we try to understand a person, we pay attention to her gestures and signs, what she says and the context in which she is operating. The context is absolutely essential. The same facial expression or utterance might have entirely different meanings in different contexts. When we say we understand someone's anger, we do not mean that we have her sensations and feel what she does. Neither do we mean that we can explain her anger in terms of traits, biology or cognitions. We mean that we recognise how her anger makes sense in her situation. Hermeneutic understanding entails recognition of an action and its significance. This is very different from causal explanations, where what are sought are the pushes and pulls of behaviour.

So understanding involves two processes: an appreciation of both the structure of an event and its context. Hermeneutic theorists emphasise that no reading can achieve a once-and-for-all version of the truth. All perception is always from a particular perspective on the text. The text is trying to tell us something, and the best we can do is to approach it with as little prejudice as we can. However, this ideal can never be fully achieved, as we always carry with us what to us seems like a natural attitude, but is in fact one that is saturated in cultural and personal assumptions. Both Dilthey and Gadamer emphasise that social tradition in which any interpretation is made. Immersed as we are in twenty-first century beliefs in human rights, we cannot help but see the Roman games as cruel rather than amusing. We cannot detach ourselves from our social world and arrive at a dispassionate appraisal of another. Since we cannot abolish our prejudices, the best we can do is to recognise them. Interpretation then involves what Gadamer (1975) refers to as 'the fusion of our horizon with that of the text'. Here we see the advocating of the reflexivity that has only recently been recognised as essential in qualitative psychological research.

Dilthey advocated a descriptive rather than an explanatory psychology, and this has been elaborated by phenomenologists. It was the hermeneutic theorists that first made the idiographic–nomothetic distinction. Whereas scientific explanation is derived from nomothetic studies that focus on general laws, hermeneutic understanding concentrates on particular cases, with all their rich diversity. This does not mean that we cannot discern general patterns and extend our analysis beyond our case studies. But both hermeneutic and phenomenological analyses begin with lived experience. What we experience is people acting in aggressive, dependent and shy ways. We do not see aggression, dependency and shyness, but abstract them from lived situations. And we do not deduce traits or build our perceptions from seeing them – it is people acting that we see. The whole perception is greater than the sum of the parts. It is a common experience to find that we either like or dislike someone without being able to put our finger on exactly what it is that leads us to this perception. This is because the perception, with its attendant meaning, comes first, and only later do we deconstruct our perceptions to find reasons for our assessment. As Rickman (1997) says, Dilthey's approach focuses on the wholeness of lived experience. If we want to investigate imagination, we should look first to people who we believe have good imaginations. We should not try to piece together a pattern based on abstracting from simpler cases – we will never get there. If we want to appreciate a text, we will never do it by learning the alphabet.

Phenomenology

In recent years we have seen a return to qualitative methods in psychology (Smith et al., 1995). These are generally either phenomenological or discourse analyses. We can see the distinction between them in the history of hermeneutics above. Discourse analysis focuses on the arguments in the text and does not consider authorial intention, while phenomenology reaches for the lived experience of the author which it considers is being communicated through the text.

Phenomenology was a radical style of philosophy that originated with the work of Husserl in the early twentieth century (Moran, 2000). The term 'phenomenology' has its roots in Kant's distinction between noumena (denoting things in the real world) and phenomena (the way in which they appear to us). This distinction between the real world and the world of appearances is one which phenomenology does not recognise. Phenomenological psychologists hold that we must focus on phenomena, the way in which the world appears to us. We can see here how PCT has a phenomenological aspect, concentrating as it does on the person's construction of events rather than on the events themselves. Kelly (1955) advocated a 'credulous approach' to clients; listening carefully for their particular sets of meaning which he saw in terms of construct systems. Phenomenology is thus concerned with understanding the way in which the world appears to us and not with trying to explain this by recourse to biological or cognitive underlying processes. Outhwaite (1975) saw phenomenology as advocating a particularly rigorous form of *verstehen*.

Phenomenologists conceived of consciousness in a way that avoided the dualisms of mind–body and person–world. Traditionally, consciousness has been thought of as residing in a person's mind. Consciousness of other people and the world in general is conveyed via the senses of the body to this internal mental apparatus. Husserl (1967, 1970) argued that consciousness and the world were always connected. You cannot think, experience fear or feel anticipation in a vacuum. You always think *about* something, are scared *of* something and look forward *to* something. The things we are conscious of cannot be separated from our experience. Our relationship with things is first and foremost practical; consciousness comes from reflection on what the world can do to or for us. He called these relationships 'intentional' and changed the focus from the world and the person to the world and the way in which it is experienced. There is no causal relationship between the world and the way it is experienced. Phenomenological psychology is primarily concerned with the way in which things are experienced, or appear. This is not caused by, but is correlated with, the world itself. So, I might be on a hotel balcony, six floors above ground level, and feel anxious as I look down. A spider on the wall or a bird flying past me is confronted with the same world, but it would presumably appear very different to them. For me, it appears frightening and I cannot separate this from the perception: it just appears as a frightening drop.

Phenomenological analysis

The problem that we have with trying to describe the way things appear is that we inevitably bring to bear our implicit theories and explanations which pervade any perception. People read meaning into situations. It has been demonstrated that when people are shown geometric forms like circles and rectangles moving on a screen, they see it as one chasing or avoiding the other. It is extremely difficult to stay with description, as we move from description to explanation. For example, we might look at two people arguing and see one of them browbeating the other. One is an aggressive person while the other is a meek victim. We can see here that it is very difficult to separate description from explanation and indeed value judgement. And the conclusions we jump to come from culturally available constructions; in this case, trait theory. As we saw in Chapter 2, people readily assign dispositions to others and screen out situational factors that might well account for what is happening. The hermeneutic theorists referred to this as 'prejudice embedded in cultural tradition'. Husserl (1970) called it 'the natural attitude'. The aim of phenomenology is to open our perception to other possibilities. We can see another similarity with Kelly here, with his advocacy of constructive alternativism.

The 'natural attitude' is the lens through which we see things, and consequently very difficult to see itself. It is the horizon, or ground, against which we make out figures in our perception. In everyday life, people assume that the way they see things is the only way. Twenty years ago, I can remember reading that a manufacturer of school canes was appalled that his products were being sold for the pleasure of 'perverts' in sex shops. He thought it perfectly OK that children were being beaten with them in schools. The tabloid newspaper that interviewed him seemed to share his indignation, as the readers were meant to do. No explanation of this paradox was deemed necessary. Yet a visitor from Sweden where corporal punishment was banned might have wondered about the assumptions behind this aspect of the natural attitude. Why is it OK to beat children and condemn sexual pleasure between consenting adults? And now, only twenty years later, one could not imagine such an interview being published in even the most reactionary tabloid, in the current climate concerning child abuse. This example neatly shows how the world always affords many more interpretations than those that are immediately apparent. Ihde (1986) demonstrates how the

Necker cube (an example of an ambiguous figure) can be viewed so as to reveal many more perceptions than the conventional two given in introductory psychological texts. With simple guidance, anyone can achieve a range of new perceptions if we can achieve *epoche*, the standing back and viewing in a way that might be adopted by a stranger who does not share the natural attitude.

It is this backdrop that forms the beginning of Berger and Luckmann's (1967) phenomenological investigation into the social construction of reality. They note that people take for granted the social world that surrounds them in much the same way that they do the physical world. The customs and social practices that you are born into come to seem as natural as the law of gravity. Yet there is nothing 'necessarily so' about social life; it can be and indeed is constructed very differently in different societies. Birth, sex and death occur everywhere but can be treated quite differently. Berger and Luckmann (1967) were interested in the way that society appears to people and how, in light of this, they reproduce and change it. Much of their work is based on that of Schutz, one of Husserl's students who immigrated to the USA from Germany. As a stranger to North American society, he had the opportunity of looking at it from the outside. This allowed the possibility of standing back from the natural attitude of those immersed in it. But achieving this phenomenological attitude is less easy in everyday life.

In order to overcome the natural attitude and promote phenomenological seeing, Husserl suggested a procedure called *epoche*. Ihde (1986) refers to this as a set of hermeneutic rules that set the focus of inquiry and shape interpretation. The steps in this procedure are bracketing, phenomenological description and horizontalisation. Suppose we wanted to conduct a phenomenological investigation into shyness. We do a literature search and find that there are many overlapping terms with slightly different definitions: shyness, social anxiety, embarrassment, social phobia and self-consciousness. There are also many theories in play, each proposing different types of cause, for example lack of social skill, biological/trait predisposition and cognitive schema. Our investigation will be phenomenological. We are interested in how the phenomenon appears to those who 'suffer' from it. So we decide to interview people who define themselves as shy. The first thing we must do is to bracket our preconceptions about shyness. So, is it always the case that it is a problem? We might remember that, up until the 1970s, homosexuality was treated by psychologists as something that needed treatment. Because shyness is described in the literature as something needing correcting or treatment, we are likely to just assume that it is problematic. Then we must aim at a phenomenological description. This means we must be careful to avoid slipping into causal explanation. People in our study may well tell us why they think they are shy. This will be part of how shyness appears to them, but certainly we must avoid questioning them about traumatic incidents, when they first recognised 'the problem' and if their parents are shy. And in our interviews we might want to try to get them to stand back as far as possible from the natural attitude in which they might give us formulaic and well-rehearsed explanations of shyness. Finally, we must make no assumptions about the relative importance of the phenomena that they report. We must resist the temptation to move the interview onto what *we* consider to be the important issues. All material must be treated with equal horizontal importance as we try to capture how things appear to the interviewee. There are many variations of phenomenological method (see Moustakas, 1994), but all emphasise the importance of first-person accounts.

Phenomenological theory has undergone many developments since Husserl's time (see Moran and Mooney, 2002). The generation that followed Husserl – Heidegger, Sartre and Merleau-Ponty – have been labelled 'existential phenomenologists'. Husserl's phenomenology began with appearances but aimed to establish the essence of different experiences. He proposed a 'transcendental ego' that constituted experience. The existentialists saw this as a return to idealism and dualism. Their central concept of existence stressed that there is no fixed nature, no essence of humankind. Instead, Sartre (1948) claimed that 'man turns up and makes something of himself'. We can see here a connection with constructionism; an emphasis on the plasticity of humankind and the perspectival nature of all perception and construction. Concepts like 'intentionality' evolved into 'being-in-the-world'. This underlines our grounding in the social world and the horizons of the human condition in lived space and time. Intersubjectivity, space and time will always be the backdrops against which our experience must be seen (Keen, 1975). Being a human body-subject, I inevitably see things against the background of these dimensions. I will now concentrate on the existential phenomenology of Merleau-Ponty, because I believe that it offers the best elaboration of being-in-the-world and the sort of psychological understanding that is the focus of this book.

Merleau-Ponty

Maurice Merleau-Ponty (1908–61) was both a philosopher and a psychologist. His early work (1963, but originally published in 1942) focused on a criticism of behaviourism and a promotion of some aspects of gestalt psychology. Between 1949 and 1952 he held the chair in child psychology at the Sorbonne, later to be occupied by Piaget. His most well-known work was *Phenomenology of Perception* (1962, but originally published in 1945), in which he criticised the idealism and dualism prevalent in philosophy and instead elaborated the concept of the body-subject. Central to this project was his critique of what he termed 'objective thought'. In considering Merleau-Ponty's work, I will look first at this critique and then at the implications of his thoughts on embodiment. We will see that out of this emerges an existential phenomenology that both complements and enriches the work of George Mead.

Objective thought and lived experience

'Objective thought' is Merleau-Ponty's term for that aspect of the modern natural attitude that comes to us mainly through our dependence on the natural sciences. This is a doctrine concerning the nature of the entities that make up the world. Science typically looks for the constituent parts of things in the world, in order to generate causal laws. In this way, psychologists have abstracted entities like emotion from the people and situations in which they occur. As Harré (1986: 4) says, from angry people, anxious parents and grieving families, psychologists have abstracted anger, anxiety and grief. Traditional psychology, as well as the phenomenology of Husserl, concentrates on these abstractions, or 'essences'. In contrast, existentialism stresses that existence precedes essence. This means that our experience is first and foremost grounded in our human perspective. And Merleau-Ponty brings us back to the way things appear to us. Using the example of a red carpet (1962: 4–5), he points out that we do not see redness as a colour except in the context of the wool of the carpet. Our perception cannot be readily broken down into constituent parts, or the combination of the essences of colour and texture. The same red would be quite different if it were a painted surface. As the gestalt psychologists showed so effectively, the whole perception is always more than the sum of the parts. But so successful has the natural science project been, that we take for granted its world view.

This separates person from world, producing a subject–object split. What is subjective and what is objective must be sharply demarcated in order for our objective knowledge of the world to be uncontaminated by subjective thoughts, feelings and opinions. This is why, in orthodox experiments, we separate 'results' (which are supposedly objective) from 'conclusions' (there the experimenter brings to bear her interpretation of the results). Objective thought holds that the world consists of separate and ultimately definable objects that obey lawful relationships. Merleau-Ponty called these 'external' relationships, by which he meant the causal relationships that may hold between separate objects. These objects are separate from each other and, of course, from the perceiving subject, who comes to know them through the physical sensations of the body. Objective thought maintains that the properties of these objects can ultimately be known and defined. The scientific venture is therefore one of discovery.

All this may be appropriate in the natural sciences. Even though the world of theoretical physics, with its relativity, quarks and super-strings, may question this simplistic formulation, most of the time natural scientists deal in terms of a real objective world. But it just will not do in the social sciences. As Berger and Luckmann (1967) argued, social reality is both a discovery *and* a construction. This both/and as opposed to either/or is the hallmark of constructivism and constructionism in psychology and considerably extends our understanding of social and personal worlds. When people are the object of study, the subjective and objective merge into one another. Orthodox psychologists, along with many in the critical social psychology camp, worry about the relativism of constructionism. When everything is dependent on a particular perspective, they say, how can we ever know anything? But Warren (1992), writing from within personal construct theory, contended that it is better to think in terms of subjecting and objecting, rather than the existence of different subjective and objective realms. Transforming these nouns into verbs stresses that, sometimes, it is important to focus on individual meanings, and sometimes to go beyond this to establish common ground. This is precisely what phenomenological investigations aim to do. They typically begin with the way things appear to individuals, and only then look for patterns, commonalities or essences of the experiences.

Merleau-Ponty argued that there were various ways in which objective thought failed to do justice to our lived experience (see Hammond et al. (1991) for an excellent summary). He ranges widely over aspects of perception to argue his case, but I will concentrate here on issues that concern personality theories. Objective thought maintains that the dimensions and properties of separate objects can be known and defined. But with psychological 'objects', for example thoughts and emotions, there can be no clear separation and definition. Nevertheless, psychologists have tried to identify primary emotions, which, like primary colours, are mixed to produce the almost infinite variety of feelings that we experience (Kaufman, 1993). But our experience of these psychological processes is fuzzy. Despite the humanistic psychologists' exhortation to 'get in touch with our feelings', it is impossible to know exactly what we are thinking or feeling by introspecting; looking inside our minds to read some imaginary internal meter. As Wittgenstein (1972) showed (and I discussed in Chapter 4), we do not have a private language to do this. When we say how we feel, we are not involved in the language game of description, but of expression. We are trying to communicate, and not accurately describing an inner world. Merleau-Ponty insisted that everything in the lived world is ambiguous, that is, open to different interpretations. So it is quite often the case that we apparently feel two supposedly incompatible emotions at the same time: love and hate, fascination and disgust, melancholy and comfort. Now, this does not mean that what we feel is somewhere in between the two, that one emotion balances the other; far from it. If we are pressed to say what we *really* feel, we will not be able to do justice to the confusing and frequently uncomfortable mixture of feelings we have.

Because the objective world is populated by separate definable entities, external causal relationships are thought to pertain between them. So as we saw in Chapter 1, personality theorists argue about the relative primacy of thought, emotion and behaviour. Which causes which? Merleau-Ponty claimed that in lived experience, there can be no firm boundaries between these psychological entities and therefore external relationships do not apply. In the physical world, we might legitimately say that it is a drop in temperature that causes water to freeze, but only because the temperature and the state of water can be separately assessed. This is not the case with thoughts, feelings and behaviour. Here, internal relations apply: each unfolds in the light of the development of the other and there is no unidirectional causality. Imagine you are greeting a friend enthusiastically. You are waving, smiling and thinking vaguely about the good times you've had together. It is not that the thoughts cause the feelings and behaviour, or that the feelings of warmth and happiness cause the thoughts and behaviour. Happiness is the whole configuration; one that makes sense and is hence understandable in this context. The mixture of feelings, cognitions and actions are internally related; that is, they are of an expressive and meaningful nature. We can see here a clear contrast with cognitive social approaches to personality, along with those cognitive therapies that are associated with them. There, cognitions are seen as being at the root of feeling and 'behaviour', and therapeutic efforts are directed at modifying fundamental cognitions.

With its clear distinction between subject and object, objective thought sees meaning as residing either in the world or in the perceiver. But Merleau-Ponty argued that the person and the world he perceives are also in internal relationship, and meaning is in neither, but arises in the interaction between the two. So when we describe the sea as angry, it is not that we think the sea feels anger, but neither is it that we project this feeling onto the sea. Projections take place whatever the nature of the object; it is merely a screen that carries our projection. But the world will not afford any construction. As Kelly (1955) said, any valid construction requires some validation when placed on the world of events. We are trying to put into words our relationship to the sea; how we must act towards it. We are saying we must be careful, must not push our luck in view of its awesome power and ability to damage us. It is to be remembered that consciousness is a matter of 'I can' and that our perceptions and constructions have a pragmatic purpose. We are not disembodied minds but body-subjects who are both in and of the world. There is no Cartesian province of the mind in which thought and speech are not intimately related to our everyday concerns.

The body-subject
It is important to note that Merleau-Ponty used the term 'subject' in a quite different way from Foucault. This is not the subject of sovereign or disciplinary power, but subject as opposed to object; the person–world dualism. In the objective thought of Descartes, the body is seen as an object, in the sense that the mind is the province of the subjective while the body is part of the objective material world. Merleau-Ponty wanted to bring the body over to the subjective side of this correlation. It is from the body that we think, feel and act. Descartes' idealism posited an internal *cogito*, a thinking being, in charge of the machinery of a body. As we saw in Chapter 1, this ghost interpreted incoming sense

data and pulled the strings of the machine accordingly. A rational reflective consciousness was the origin of human life. This idea brought science into line with the dualistic dogma of Christianity, and formed the basis of the modern view of people as essentially rational. Macquarrie (1972) points out that the hallmark of existentialism is a shift from the thinking subject of Cartesian dualism to the subject as agent. It begins with the person not as a reflective thinker, but as an engaged actor. As an existential phenomenologist, Merleau-Ponty's proposition was that consciousness was primarily a matter of 'I can' rather than 'I think'. Our connection with the world is first and foremost a practical one; our relationship to it is in terms of what it can do to or for us. When I sit in front of my keyboard, my practical concern with it overrides all others and guides my perception of it. I glance at it from time to time, checking with the monitor that my typing is OK. If someone asked me to write out the layout of letters on the keyboard, I couldn't do it. I have not learned and reflected on this layout, it is enough that my fingers can use it more or less effectively. Similarly, I could not tell you how I walk or ride a bicycle. All this is not the work of a *cogito* – an internal thinker – but of a lived body or body-subject, whose connection with the world is primarily pre-reflective and practical. The cognitive reflective functions of consciousness are a subsequent development.

Merleau-Ponty used the example of the phantom limb to underline the powers of the body-subject. This phenomenon sometimes occurs when someone loses a limb as a result of an accident or surgery. She might find that she still experiences pain in the limb or, even more distressingly, acts as though the limb were still intact. Both materialist and idealist explanations of this phenomenon are unsatisfactory. The limb is not there to transmit sensation, and the person knows it is missing. Nevertheless, the experience is real enough. As a phenomenologist, Merleau-Ponty did not seek an explanation, but an understanding of the experience. He argued that we pre-reflectively draw on a plan of our body all the time. If someone throws a ball to you, you are likely to try to catch it before you can think or say what you have done. No deliberation is necessary. Indeed, as anyone playing ball games knows, time to think often makes for a worse move. Our present body draws on a body plan in order to connect practically with its day-to-day tasks. The phantom limb phenomenon shows this clearly. Here, Merleau-Ponty was rethinking the concept of habit:

it is the body which understands the acquisition of habit. This way of putting it will appear absurd, if understanding is subsuming a sense-datum
under an idea and if the body is regarded as an object. But the phenomenon of habit is just what prompts us to revise our notion of 'understand'
and our notion of the body. (1962: 144)

So the body is not under the control of a mind. It is not, as Merleau-
Ponty calls it, 'Descartes' dummy'. Neither, as Skinner (1974)
claimed, is it under the control of the environment (although his formulation has more in common with phenomenology, because it does
not posit a mind within a body). Rather, the body interacts with the
world, both finding and constructing meaning within it.

   In order to demonstrate how we take for granted the body's practical hold on the world, Merleau-Ponty (1962) drew extensively on the
case study of a World War I veteran called Schneider. Schneider had
suffered damage to the occipital lobes of his brain; that part normally
associated with vision. However, his vision was more or less intact. But
he had lost much of the ability to orient himself in time and space.
So this case study shows how some practical consciousness remained
after the brain damage, although Schneider was no longer aware of
his body's position in space in the way that we accept as normal.
So, with his eyes closed, he only knew if he was standing upright by
paying attention to the pressure of the ground on the soles of his feet.
He was unable to point to his nose, although he could scratch it when
it itched. The loss of what Merleau-Ponty called 'abstract thought'
meant that he could not project himself imaginatively beyond his
immediate situation. People are part of what Merleau-Ponty called
the 'human order', as well as the 'vital order' (Merleau-Ponty, 1963).
All life is part of the vital order, a level of organisation that is common
to all living things. Even here, simple causal relationships do not
apply as they do in the 'physical order', between inanimate objects.
But humankind deals with the world in terms of symbols and meanings, not just stimuli and responses; a point echoed by Mead and the
symbolic interactionists who were inspired by him. When we see a
sign reading 'No Smoking', we know it is not a description but an
instruction. This is only because we inhabit a symbolic universe and
share a set of common meanings with others. We recognise the sign as
made up of linguistic symbols and can immediately recognise what it
means. Schneider had lost this ability. Merleau-Ponty argued that in
humankind, everything is both natural and cultural; it is impossible
to separate the two. This means that the body-subject simultaneously

inhabits both vital and human orders. They are not different realms, where one can be reduced to the other, but different ways of talking about the same thing (or, in Kellian terms, alternative constructions of the same events). But participation in the human order transforms the simple descriptions that belong to the vital order. So, for example, sexuality is at the same time a natural, cultural and personal function. When we hear people say that 'sex is mainly in the head', they mean that it is not just a matter of mere sensation; it has meaning. But for Schneider, it had lost meaning. Although he was not impotent, he never initiated sexual activity. He would participate in it, but not be bothered if it was suddenly interrupted.

The use of the Schneider case is rather like the breaching experiments that we looked at in Chapter 4. Phenomenologists often help us achieve *epoche* by using extraordinary cases that draw our attention to what we take for granted in the ordinary. The properties of human embodiment are such that we have invented the mind to account for them. We should really talk about being bodies rather than having them, but we are so imbued with the natural attitude of dualism that we think of the body as inanimate machinery inhabited by Ryle's spectral presence. Like the other existentialists, Merleau-Ponty argued that we should think of ourselves in terms of being-in-the-world; part of a system from which we are inseparable:

> [The world] is the natural setting of, and field for, all my thoughts and all my explicit perceptions. Truth does not 'inhabit' only the 'inner man', or more accurately, there is no inner man, man is in the world, and only in the world does he know himself. (1962: xi)

The natural attitude leads us to accept uncritically that consciousness is in our heads. But with just a little thought we realise that it is normally outside ourselves, caught up in our day-to-day activities. When you are watching a film, talking to people or engrossed in a game, you are not normally conscious of yourself at all. There is just the world and the way in which you experience it. As I said in the previous section, Merleau-Ponty thought of people as in internal relation with the world, particularly the social world. Meaning resides between body-subjects rather than within them. I will have more to say about this in subsequent chapters, since it is crucial in understanding ourselves and others. Now, I want to turn to a discussion of George Mead's social psychology. This can be seen as complementing and extending the insights of existential phenomenology.

Mead's social psychology

Mead was a leading figure in American pragmatism. This was a philosophical movement that developed in the USA in the early twentieth century (Thayer, 1982). It has many parallels (but also differences in emphases) with phenomenology, which flourished in Europe during the same period. It grounds meaning in human action and is anti-Cartesian. It influenced education, the arts and social policy, and through Kelly it also had an impact on psychological therapy. Mead was a friend and colleague of John Dewey (on whose work Kelly based PCT), and we can detect Mead's influence on PCT, principally in Kelly's sociality corollary. Mead had studied briefly in Germany at the turn of the twentieth century and, as a student of both Wundt and Dilthey, he incorporated the spirit of *verstehen* in his pragmatism. An understanding of human action always entails an appreciation of its social context and construction. His focus was on the social act; how action is conducted in the light of others' perspectives and meanings. He was strongly influenced by the evolutionary theory of Darwin and saw human consciousness as an emergent property (Joas, 1985). In contrast to Descartes, for whom a reflective consciousness is the origin of human action, Mead saw it as rooted in organismic processes. His proposition was that consciousness was something that humankind had evolved in order to aid cooperative ventures and the social cohesion that were responsible for the species' success. He distinguished between physical, vital and mental levels of organisation. There is a striking similarity here with Merleau-Ponty's (1963) physical, vital and human orders (Rosenthal and Bourgeois, 1991). Physical systems do not necessarily involve life, and life does not necessarily involve mental functioning. Emergence is defined as partaking in more than one system, where higher levels of organisation transform lower. This is the exact opposite of the reductionism prevalent in contemporary psychology, where higher functioning is supposedly explained in terms of lower. We are told that there is a gene for love and homosexuality and that spirituality is hard-wired. But these reductionist explanations do not provide satisfactory explanations for human action. No one gasps in awe when they are told that Westminster Abbey is really just made out of stones; we recognise that the whole is greater than the sum of the parts. Similarly, consciousness cannot be explained in neurological terms. Of course we need neurones to think, but explanation at this level is not sufficient. Mead argued that the agentic and reflective processes that characterise the self evolved through the interaction with others that was necessary for survival.

The social act

Mead contended that all aspects of human intelligence and consciousness have their roots in simple organic processes (Mead, 1982a). In the vital order, all living things anticipate and adapt to the environment; there is never the simple unidirectional stimulus–response relationship posited by behaviourists. Animals signal to each other using gestures. Combinations of gestures can lead to complicated joint patterns, for example mating rituals. The beginning of an act on the part of one individual produces a complementary act on the part of another, which in its turn produces new action developments. In lower animals, these may be fixed action patterns, but higher up the evolutionary scale there are more flexible conversations of gestures. What marked out the human order for Mead was the extent of the elaboration of the conversation of gestures, and its evolution into language. He claimed that it was social cooperation that was the motor for this development. Imagine two people signalling to each other about an imminent danger, one they can together overcome. There is an important difference between mere signals and a symbolic significance of the signs used. Birds often signal each other at the approach of a cat, whereupon all birds in the vicinity take flight. But this is very different from one person conveying to another: 'Here's a fierce dog. We'll never outrun him, but if we both stand our ground, pick up these sticks, he might not attack. If he does, he'll only be able to go for one of us at a time, and the other one can beat his brains out.' It's immediately obvious that a common language is an enormous advantage in communication. But one can imagine an exercise of mime where one individual sees what the other is driving at.

In a conversation of gestures, the early stages of an act produce another phase of the joint act in another individual. There are two phases of the social act: an overt phase in which one party moves, and a covert phase in which the other interprets and makes sense of the act, then responds in the beginning of another overt phase. So how the social act ends is not determined at the beginning of the sequence – it is a joint product in which each individual responds pre-reflectively, moment by moment as the dance proceeds. It is this that Blumer (1969) and later Shotter (1993) refer to as 'joint action'. An important transition in this process occurs when individuals find themselves checking their own behaviour in the light of the responses of the other. Suppose you find yourself in a group of people, telling a joke that you realise is not being well received. You might experience feelings of anxiety, irritation or frustration. But you decide it's not worth offending the company, and draw back from saying anything too provocative. This involves a complex exercise in sociality and self-control. It involves putting yourself into the shoes of others and seeing yourself reflected in their eyes. In Kelly's terms, you construe their constructions and play a role with respect to them. The only reason this does not seem extraordinarily complicated is that we do it all the time and thus take the process for granted. We view ourselves from others' perspectives, conduct inner dialogues and carry on joint action without much deliberation. We develop the ability to reflect on our action, and we become both an 'I' and a 'me'; an agent and an object of our own reflection. It is this process that Mead refers to as 'self' (Mead, 1982b). For both Mead and Merleau-Ponty, the self is decentred, that is, it is not an inner essence but a social construction (Rosenthal and Bourgeois, 1991). While the self-process is largely implicit in Merleau-Ponty's work, it is more fully theorised in Mead's.

Self

Mead's theory is the exact opposite of the individualism in orthodox psychology and personality theory. In the tradition of Cartesian dualism, psychology generally starts with the individual self and tries to explain how these social atoms come together to form society. Mead begins with society and people's connection with each other and tries to explain how individual selves are formed. This is clearly a version of social constructionism, but one that conceives of an individual that, once constructed, is a centre for choice and agency. Individuals are not subject to discourses or moved passively around in the field of ideology. Each person is an 'I', a genuine source of action that, in Berger and Luckmann's terms, externalises. The self is not an inner essence that predates social interaction, but a process of reflection on one's action, a 'me'.

In trying to understand how the social world becomes a reality for the individual, Berger and Luckmann (1967) drew on Mead's account of primary socialisation. This involves the development of the self through the construing of the constructions of significant others, such as parents. In the conversation of gestures, and later language, the child comes to see herself from the perspective of her parents, adopting their meanings towards her acts. In this way, an 'objective' set of meanings is internalised. This, of course, is a pre-reflective process that takes place without conscious thought and reflection. In secondary socialisation, the self-process is elaborated when social acts are conducted with a range of others. This involves the taking on of multiple perspectives and role relationships.

I have already argued (Chapter 1) that much of modern academic psychology can be thought of as 'not Mead'. This is because when Watson, Mead's PhD student at Chicago, joined the experimental psychology department, he distanced himself from Mead's philosophy (see Farr, 1996). Consequently, most psychologists today think of Mead as a philosopher or a sociologist. His standing as a sociologist comes from his adoption as a key figure by the symbolic interactionists. The term 'symbolic interactionism' was coined by Herbert Blumer (1969), a Chicago sociologist who drew on George Mead and others to produce an interpretive sociology. In a similar way, the main tenets of symbolic interactionism can be seen as a response to Watson's behaviourism. Watson claimed that the reflex arc was the unit of analysis that psychologists should build upon. People responded to stimuli without any mediating cognition. There was no place at all for thought or imagery in Watson's psychology. In contrast, symbolic interactionism stressed that we act towards things on the basis of meanings they have for us, that this meaning is derived from interaction with others, and that internal dialogue and thought mediated and modified the nature of this meaning. This is basically a cognitive approach, and the proposition that we act in the light of meanings that are cognitively mediated should not seem foreign to contemporary psychologists. However, the proposition that meaning is derived from interaction will seem odd to psychologists embedded in an individualistic approach to the person. But as we have seen, this idea can be traced to the work of Mead, work that has, sadly, been ignored by psychologists.

A synthesis

Interpretive sociology – phenomenology and symbolic interactionism – has been particularly important in opening our perception to different perspectives. It has introduced us to the way other people see things, without attempting to justify or explain these different constructions. Surely, this ought to be the project of a science of ʌality. It ought to help us understand others who do not share ʌorld view. Let us now put together the idea of personality that emᴗᴗges in existential phenomenology.

Pre-reflective consciousness

The person is not a ghost inside a machine: a mind inside a body. Instead, the body-subject is essentially an animal that has evolved a reflective ability out of what is primarily a practical, pre-reflective consciousness. 'Consciousness' in this sense merely means 'awake' rather than 'asleep'. Like any animals, we are first and foremost in the business of staying alive. This involves avoiding threats, getting food and shelter and mating. This is Merleau-Ponty's (1962: 137) 'I can' rather than 'I think' as a basis for human life; the participation in a vital order that doesn't require deliberation and thought. In the natural run of everyday life, we are not self-conscious but, as it were, outside ourselves and caught up in our different projects. As I ride a bike, try to make a tennis shot or write, it is as if I were *in* the bike, the tennis racquet or the screen I am looking at. I don't have to think about myself doing it, just as I don't have to think about what I am going to say before I say it. My words seem to form the thoughts as they come out. If I do try to watch myself, paradoxically, I make a worse tennis shot, am more likely to fall off the bike or get tongue-tied. I don't usually have to make my body do things; it just does them. As Kelly (1955: 48) put it, the person is a form of motion – we find our body doing the things we want to do. Of course, I can try to make it work in a particular way, or try to stop it doing some things, but this is the exception rather than the rule, and just underlines how we don't normally act like minds working bodies. The body, as it were, has a mind of its own. Indeed, this is the only 'mind' we have!

Meaning is co-constituted in interaction

Meanings do not reside in the world, but neither are they read into it and the result of the projections of a mind. Instead, they are the result of the pre-reflective interaction between the person and the world. If I see a person as sexually attractive, threatening or interesting, it is not that they *really* are or are not sexy, threatening or interesting; these properties do not in any simple way reside in the person. We might give them a personality inventory to fill in, but this wouldn't settle the issue. All we will discover is what they think about themselves, and who is to say that they are right and not deluding themselves? So is it that these traits, like beauty, are in the eye of the beholder? Is it all my projection of meaning? Not exactly. There has to be something in the other person that I am responding to and anticipating. For a start, we are talking about a person. I can't find my reading lamp interesting, sexy or threatening, and doubt that anyone could. Neither is it the opposite, uninteresting, kind or non-sexy; it is outside the range of these dichotomous constructs. The meanings we appear to find in or attribute to things and other people are the product of our interaction (or imagined interaction) with them. As Mead argued: 'The feelings of readiness to take up or read a book, to spring over a ditch, to hurl a stone, are the stuff out of which arises the meaning of the book, the ditch and the stone' (1982a: 343). The 'I can' of pre-reflective consciousness produces meaning between us and things or events in the world. And, of course, things can become saturated with the meaning we construe in people. My dad's pen, the card my daughter gave me and the book I have forgotten to return to my friend all have something about these particular people in them.

When we interact with other people, the conversation of gestures that ensues produces joint action for which neither individual is solely responsible. One of the properties of human embodiment is that we read others' intentions in minute cues that we are often unable to describe. This 'intuition' leads to us anticipating their reactions and acting in the light of them. It is this interpretation of others that leads to the production of a reflective consciousness.

Reflective consciousness

With other people, how we feel, think and act towards them affects how they construe us. Again, Mead sums this up very nicely:

> We are conscious of our attitudes because they are responsible for the changes in the conduct of other individuals. A man's reaction towards weather conditions has no influence upon the weather itself. It is important for the success of his conduct that he should be conscious not of his own attitudes, of his own habits of response, but of the signs of rain or fair weather. Successful social conduct brings one into a field within which a consciousness of one's own attitudes helps toward the control of the conduct of others. (Mead, 1982a: 348)

'Consciousness' here means more than just the being awake of pre-reflective consciousness. It refers to the way we deliberate upon

things and, in particular, on our own action, regulating it as a consequence. This consciousness is the product of sociality, and it is in this
sense that the person is a social construction. It is through social practices, and in particular language, that we develop the ability to
reflect on things. This involves transforming our situation imaginatively, turning over possibilities and conducting inner dialogues.
This is the human order to which both Merleau-Ponty and Mead
refer. Language provides us with the tools with which to think, but
also shapes our thinking. It is not just a toolbox we dip into in order
to express pre-reflective thoughts and feelings. There is no essence
inside us awaiting expression; as Merleau-Ponty put it, language is
the body and not the clothing of our thought. We make our thoughts
in what we are saying.

But experience is a complicated mixture of making and finding,
discovery and construction. It refers to a real world of experience, a
pre-reflective engagement that powers language and at the same
time is shaped by it. Although for each individual, a pre-reflective
infancy precedes a reflective life, once language is used, it forms as
well as is formed by the pre-reflective realm. It gives us the ability to
reflect on things, and particularly on our own action, from the perspective of others.

The self-process

It is in this way that the process of self develops. The self is not a cognitive entity; a structure that is at the centre of the person and which
precedes interaction with others. It is a process of reflection that is
the outcome of this interaction. Consequently, we do not each possess
a unitary 'real' or 'true' self. As a process rather than a structure, the
self is open to constant change. However, early layers that we have
laid down, perhaps as the outcome of interactions with our carers,
might appear most authentic and fundamental to us. Harré commented (1989) that to have a self means nothing more than to have a
self-theory. But a theory has consequences. As Kelly (1955) claimed,
the anticipatory stance we take up on the world is based on our different theories about it. And surely no aspect of the world is more important than our own action. Others judge and react to us on the basis
of it. We know this very well and adjust accordingly in Mead's social
action. This 'me' aspect of the self-process is a social construction and
a theory that we rely on to relate to others. Of course this is a silent
theory. Kelly was not saying that this was a formal theory, logically

derived and deliberated upon. We may well not be aware of our theoretical presuppositions and, to this extent, they are unconscious and perhaps all the more powerful.

But there is another aspect of the self-process: an 'I' or agent that is never entirely captured in reflection. What I do pre-reflectively appears to me filtered through the theory of myself that I have constructed. It will be open to some interpretations and not others. There are some things I will miss, not picked out in the searchlight of my particular theory. And perhaps there are some things I do that I would prefer not to see, and so look the other way. Like Nelson holding his telescope to his blind eye, I might see no meanness or spite in what I do. But I am nonetheless a centre for moral choice and agency. Even though I can't be certain where every course of action will lead (particularly if it involves others where joint action might take over), I bear some responsibility for what I do. I am not just a ping-pong ball, bouncing off the contingencies of reinforcement or washed along in the tide of discourse.

This approach to the person leads us to rethink the questions about personality that I outlined in Chapter 1. This isn't surprising. Questions such as 'are the causes of behaviour internal or external?' are predicated on a science of personality that seeks explanations in terms that make no sense in the light of existential phenomenology. Here, the aim of the game is not causal explanation but interpretive understanding. In the next four chapters, I will consider some of the issues raised in Chapter 1 from the perspective of existential phenomenology.

6

The Causes of Behaviour

As I noted in Chapter 1, personality theories have focused on individual differences; on how and why it is that we have such different tastes
and interests. This issue has been seen traditionally in terms of internal
versus external causes of behaviour. Pervin and John (2001) see Freud
and Skinner as occupying extreme positions on a person versus situation dimension. Now, they say, personality theorists accept the importance of both, and concentrate on the interaction between the person
and the situation. Now, it's certainly important to realise that this is a
complicated issue (and, of course, both Freud and Skinner recognised
this). But the mistake is to think that causal relationships operate at
all, only in a more complicated way. This idea is predicated upon Cartesian dualism, which separates the material world of the body, other
people and situations from the mind, with its cognitions and affects.
The question then arises: does the mind substance cause the person to
act, or are people at the mercy of materialist forces in the environment? This internal world is sometimes mapped in terms of the self
or, alternatively, unconscious forces. Whether forces acting on the
individual are seen as external or internal, they are still forces that
motivate or energise the person, explaining why they do one thing
rather than another. We do not have to subscribe to this internal
versus external division. In Kelly's terms, this a bipolar construct
that channels our thinking in a more or less useful way. We, the
construers, are responsible for it and it does not necessarily tell us
anything about how the world is actually structured. My contention
is that it is definitely not a useful distinction. In this chapter, I will
consider the issues of what is thought of as 'external' causation: the
effects of the past, especially past trauma and the present situations
in which we find ourselves. Then in Chapter 7, I will focus on what

is seen as 'internal' mental life – the province of the self and the dynamic unconscious.

The influence of the past

Many people imagine that when visiting a psychotherapist, the assessment and therapy will focus on the unearthing of long-lost memory that has somehow eaten away at them and caused psychological disturbance. Popular film and TV shows encourage this idea. An expert delves into the depths of the person, extracting some memory or other, and the psychic abscess is lanced. Frequently the trauma is some sort of sexual abuse. Understanding people here translates into recognising what has happened to them. Psychological backing for this comes from both ends of the therapeutic spectrum. Since Freud's work over a hundred years ago, it has been accepted that what happens to us in childhood has its effects on adult development. And the behaviourists argued that many problems based on anxiety – phobias, obsessions and compulsions – could be explained by traumatic conditioning, that is, the pairing of a neutral with a fear-provoking stimulus. Although the classical psychoanalysts and the behaviourists used quite different vocabularies, both saw distressing emotional experience as being caused by traumatic events. And both emphasised irrationality in the development of disturbance. Conditioning occurred at a subcortical level that bypassed rational thought and unconscious forces paid little heed to reason.

Yet it was not until 1980 that the syndrome of post-traumatic stress disorder (PTSD) was officially defined in the Diagnostic and Statistical Manual for Mental Disorders (DSM) (American Psychiatric Association, 1994). The DSM has been subject to several revisions, each attempting to refine psychiatric knowledge. New disorders are added and others deleted. It is interesting to note that although psychiatrists claim to 'discover' new illnesses in the same way that physical medicine does, one can see the processes of cultural influence and social construction in successive elaborations of the DSM. So homosexuality was seen as a mental illness until 1974, when it was voted out in the wake of legal reform concerning gay sexuality. And the dreadful effects of battle stress were clearly evident long before the advent of PTSD, although they were treated as cowardice or lack of moral fibre. The symptoms of PTSD are:

- *Intrusion.* The sufferer is said to constantly re-experience the trauma. This re-experience is said to differ in kind from just remembering.

It is claimed that it is as though the trauma were actually happening again. The film metaphor of 'flashbacks' is used to describe this aspect of experience.

- *Avoidance*. Sufferers avoid situations that might trigger the intense emotions associated with flashbacks. Their preoccupation with the trauma also leads to an avoidance of intimacy and contact; a 'numbing' of feeling. The connection may be unconscious and lead to depression.
- *Hyperarousal*. Heightened anxiety, irritability and emotional explosiveness are said to be characteristic, leading to insomnia, depression and self-medication, that is, taking alcohol or other drugs to numb the distress.

For PTSD to be diagnosed, the patient has to have experienced or witnessed a threat to life or safety. The DSM says that it has been called 'shell shock' or 'battle fatigue syndrome' (American Psychiatric Association, 1994). Although it was once thought to be confined to war veterans, 'we now know that that PTSD also affects both female and male civilians, and that it strikes more females than males' (American Psychiatric Association website).

PTSD and objective thought

The case of PTSD nicely illustrates how the understanding of psychological distress is so firmly rooted in objective thought. Objective thought, it will be remembered, is the assumption that the world consists of discrete entities that can ultimately be defined and measured objectively; furthermore, that causal relationships can be discovered in relation to them. It is significant that the terms 'trauma' and 'stress' both have their origins in the physical world. 'Stress' comes from the world of engineering, where it denotes the forces acting on material that might cause damage. 'Trauma' is used in medicine to denote the impact of something on the body and causing damage. These metaphors have been adopted because they chime with the mechanistic and causal assumptions of objective thought, whereby trauma 'impacts' on the person, or the person is 'under' stress.

In psychology, objective thought leads us to define entities like trauma objectively, from an observer's point of view, and search for its cause. There are several points of interest to note in relation to this. The first is the tone of the quote above relating 'the facts' about PTSD. 'We now know' is very much the language of scientific discovery. There is no possibility here that science consists of the devising of alternative constructions that are to be tested for their utility. No, this is accumulative fragmentalism, what Kelly called the 'collecting of nuggets of truth'. Whenever we see the phrase 'we now know that', we should remind ourselves that we once knew that illnesses were caused by the night air and homosexuality was a mental illness. As the pragmatists insisted, knowledge is *always* provisional, a construction that is always subject to revision in the light of new theories and paradigms. We can never get to look at the real world without it being filtered through our constructions of it, and these are infused with the natural attitude of our time. Of course we see *from* these constructions and this attitude and, like the fish in its water, are blinded to the fact that there is a medium between us and the world, refracting our perceptions. In objective thought, science is a matter of discovery, not a balance of discovery and invention.

Then there is the way the quote describes the occurrence of PTSD; it is something that 'strikes'. Like the plague and natural disasters, psychological distress strikes people down. Sometimes flooding occurs and we are just unlucky to get caught up in it, or lightening strikes and is explained away as an act of God. In the same way, PTSD hits some people and not others. Not everyone exposed to the same objective trauma suffers the symptoms of PTSD. Perhaps, in the fullness of time, 'we will know' exactly why this is. Eysenck's early research on battle fatigue was aimed at explaining just this, in terms of biologically based differences in personality. PTSD will be likely to strike those unlucky enough to have an overactive autonomic nervous system. But there is no hint that the development of PTSD might have something to do with the particular way things appear and what things mean to them. Instead, the objective thought in which the psychiatric diagnostic enterprise is set dictates that an objective definition of trauma be sought, one without any reference to contaminating subjective interpretation. And so it is defined objectively; legitimate trauma is defined as some event that is life or safety threatening. An earlier version of the DSM had defined trauma even more narrowly in objective terms: as the encounter with events outside the range of normal experience. This was revised because threats to life and safety cannot be thought of as within this range. But surely, any attempt to define the experience of trauma objectively is doomed to failure. The definition must be phenomenological – in terms of how something appears to the person. We must sacrifice objectivity in order to gain an understanding of personal meaning. I once saw a woman whose partner suddenly left her for another. It came as a total shock to learn that for years he had been leading a parallel life when she thought everything was just fine at home. She couldn't get the shock of his telling her out of her mind, and was certainly numbed and hypersensitive. Yet she could not be diagnosed as having PTSD because she had not encountered an event that was threatening to life or safety.

One problem that arises when an objective definition is unrealistically insisted upon is that we are likely to focus upon the wrong types of remedy. So, 'what we now know', apparently, is that PTSD is likely to 'strike' women rather than men. We can imagine this 'fact' being used to prevent women in the military being allowed to take part in any activity that might result in exposure to combat. But perhaps women are not more fragile than men and not more likely to break down under stress. Perhaps the apparently high incidence in women is related to them being more likely to admit to both themselves and others that they are distressed. Men are far less likely to complain of all types of psychological distress like anxiety, depression and feelings of inadequacy. It is quite likely that this is because they are in a masculine culture that renders such suffering less acceptable. They are both less willing and less able to reflect on their pre-reflective feelings and experience. But we must not equate this with an absence of suffering. An understanding of PTSD that is framed in terms of obstacles to and difficulties in reflection and articulation has very different implications from those framed in objective thought. It leads us to think about how we might help and facilitate such reflection.

Understanding trauma

So understanding the effect of past events is something that can never be achieved by attempting objectively to define trauma. Of course, most people would find exposure to serious risk disturbing, but not everyone would experience the same consequences. Frankle's (1978) account of his imprisonment in Nazi concentration camps is a good example of this. It is hard to imagine a more terrifying and trauma-inducing environment. The system was designed to completely dehumanise prisoners. There were absolutely no comforts and no recourse to any of the physical and social supports that we take for granted in the modern world from which the prisoners came. There was no privacy at any time; for example all toilet activities had to be conducted in full view of the guards. Casual and institutional violence was an everyday occurrence and death an ever-present spectacle and personal threat. And yet Frankle reported extraordinary differences in prisoners' responses to all this. His conclusion was that those who survived were those who managed to maintain a sense of meaning and identity in their lives. They preserved a sense of themselves as agents who had at least some control over what happened to them. Making some sense of what was happening to them gave them a way of anticipating the future. This survival strategy of dealing with trauma has been identified in other extreme situations. Cohen and Taylor (1976) emphasised it as a successful strategy in long-term prisoners, and Snow and Anderson (2002) detail the struggle of the homeless to make sense of their plight.

Sewell (1997), working in a personal construct framework, also argues that the active ingredient in trauma is the disruption of personal meaning and identity. Drawing on his clinical work, principally with veterans of the Vietnam War, he contends that those people who suffer from PTSD are those who can make no sense of what has happened to them. Drawing on Kelly (1955), he argues that each person develops a theory of the past that helps him to make sense of the present and anticipate the future. This theory, or construct system, is not just an intellectual construction, but a practical framework that gives us a foothold on life. A central domain of this theory concerns the self; a personal narrative that gives us a sense of self over time and in different situations. Psychological trauma occurs when the person loses this sense. Some things happen to us that occasion 'constructive bankruptcy' – the inability to plot the event in terms of our system of meaning. Soldiers who have experienced or committed atrocities frequently find that their actions just do not seem to belong to them. They cannot be assimilated and hence are constantly re-experienced in an attempt to make sense of them. Sewell (1997) identifies three constructive strategies that are then open to the traumatised person. Firstly, he may dissociate – repress, forget or deny the traumatic incident, basing his sense of self on a pre-traumatised self. Secondly, he may scrap his past system of construction and see everything in terms of the trauma; everything becomes dangerous. Thirdly, he may just constrict his thinking and activities, become depressed and refuse to face the world at all.

Orthodox accounts of trauma see them as 'impacting' on people, causing more or less damage, depending on the material they hit. This may be defined in terms of biologically determined traits, or belief systems, that cannot cope with the impact. But an understanding of a traumatic event involves seeing it from the traumatised person's point of view. It is the interpretation of the event that matters, rather than the event itself. With this phenomenological approach, we are concerned with how the event appears to the person and how he makes sense of it. The lived world is ambiguous and open to many interpretations, not just those that jump out at us, the external observers.

PTSD and the social world

PTSD offers us a good example of how psychological distress cannot be understood purely at the level of the individual. In everyday life, there is much more discussion of stress and trauma than there was in the recent past. People now talk much more about being 'stressed out', 'abused' and 'traumatised'. Here we can see that the psychiatric vocabulary has infused everyday speech and concepts, with people drawing on it to make sense of their experience. People have always been abused, stressed and subject to trauma. In fact, if you think of what life must have been like in even the recent past, it must have been much more stressful than it is today. Yet people did not express themselves in these terms. The chances of RAF aircrew meeting a terrible death in Britain in World War II were horrifically high. But the men tried to keep their feelings to themselves, and what interviews there are with survivors show how denial and stoicism were the only ways of coping. 'We just got on with it, it was the only thing you could do' was one characteristic quote I noticed in a recent TV documentary in which war veterans were interviewed. It is interesting to contrast this with TV interviews with Gulf War pilots fifty years later in 1991. Pilots talked of their terror and excitement, a kaleidoscope of mixed emotion that tumbled over them in the course of action.

How are we to understand this change in expression? Surely it cannot be that pilots now have more emotional personalities than in the past. Aircrew are now carefully screened and trained in a way that was quite impossible in World War II. So this change cannot be explained in terms of individual personalities. But neither can it be that there is more stress in combat flying now; quite the reverse. Men were put in the air with minimal training and faced a high probability of a painful death in their first operation. Now, selection and training are excellent and losses minimal. To understand this transformation, we need to appreciate the difference in social climates from which these men came. We now live in a society that values stoicism much less. Instead, we are encouraged to 'get in touch with our feelings', express our feminine side and be honest with ourselves. The extraordinary rise in the popularity of psychotherapy and counselling testifies to this different way of thinking about ourselves. So individuals are different because society is different. And, of course, society is different because it is made up of different individuals. Here is Berger and Luckmann's dialectic in operation. People are born into a society that they accept as natural. But they are not just passive recipients, uncritically absorbing the discourses that make up society. They make additions and modifications, producing a new social world that others are then born into. The contemporary social world has elaborated discourses of human rights and equal opportunities. It is strongly affected by the theories of psychology and psychotherapy, and draws on their vocabularies constantly. Individuals then both make and find themselves in this world, giving expression to pre-reflective experiences that they might formerly have dismissed as cowardly, or chosen to ignore completely.

PTSD has not simply been discovered by psychologists and psychiatrists through their careful studies of individual patients. It is both a discovery and a social construction. Many more people will now feel justified in seeking professional help after the effects of trauma than will have been the case fifty years ago, when they would have been told to pull themselves together. The pre-reflective feelings that would once have been dismissed as 'nerves', a weak constitution or 'lack of moral fibre' are now read by people as the results of being psychologically shaken. They will have seen reports on TV and in the newspapers of counsellors being on hand to help everybody within a several-mile radius of a murder. They will interpret their experience within this new framework. It is a social construction; a useful one, but a construction nonetheless.

The effects of the situation

When personality theorists talk of situation-specificity, it is usually with the social context of behaviour and its interpretation that they are concerned. Mischel (1993: 543) distinguishes between the nominal and the psychological situation. The nominal situation may be a mealtime, being in the playground or watching TV. The psychological situation is at a more micro-level. So, while in front of the TV, a child may be teased by his siblings, praised by his mother or warned by his father. The resultant behaviour is then conceptualised as the product of a complex interaction between situation and person variables. The fine grain of the situation – being teased or warned – interacts with person variables. These are to do with the way the person construes the situation. So the way he encodes it ('I'm being teased'), his competencies ('I can give as good as I get'), how he values the outcome ('I have to come out on top') and his self-control strategies ('I can't stand it') all contribute to the final common pathway of behaviour. This is summed up by the 'if . . . then' analysis of the person and the situation I mentioned in Chapter 2 (*if* Tom is teased, *then* he always overreacts). Mischel's cognitive social approach is clearly an advance on the blunt instrument of trait theory. Here, Tom would get a score on an aggression scale that might ignore his entirely different behaviour in other social contexts. The cognitive social learning approach makes some attempt to work out how individuals interpret situations, and Mischel draws here on Kelly's personal construct theory. But he sees Kelly's theory as part of an early phase of 'grand theories' in personality, which has been superseded by micro-analytic approaches that are more able to recognise the complexity of behaviour (Mischel, 1993).

This move towards breaking wholes down into their constituent parts is characteristic of natural science investigations, where we find out how things work by discovering mechanisms that govern interactions at an ever-more molecular level. But this strategy can only succeed if the parts are separate from each other and causal relationships apply between them. The cognitive social approach is built not only on a dualism that separates subject from object, but the Cartesian separation of cognitive structures from body. The person is essentially a processor of information about situations, who reaches decisions and then presses the switch that sets the body into motion. But social acts do not follow this neat and logical sequence.

A phenomenological analysis

Merleau-Ponty (1964) drew on studies of infant development to argue that social interaction cannot be adequately described in this simple sequential way. He draws our attention to how, in Cartesian thinking, we deduce other people's thoughts, feelings and intentions by reasoning through analogy. When we see someone smiling warmly, we assume that he is contented, relaxed and means us no harm, because that is what it means to us when we smile. So we deduce his mental state through an analogy with our own. Of course, we do not go through this reasoning carefully and deliberately. Presumably, the thought processes have 'gone underground', in the same way that childhood thinking begins as overt speech and evolves into silent tele-graphed inner dialogues. This is the way that the cognitive therapists like Meichenbaum (1977) believe that thinking and reasoning develop in the infant. When you conceive of cognition as an internal mental activity that has to be inferred from behaviour, how else can it be that we understand other people? Because our natural attitude is so thoroughly infused with the Cartesian assumption of minds inside bodies, we find it difficult to reason in any other way.

But an observation of very young infants demonstrates that they certainly do not employ this reasoning by analogy. A baby smiles when an adult smiles at him – he returns the gesture unthinkingly. He cannot be reflecting in the manner the dualist claims, because he does not have separate knowledge of what his feelings are, and what he looks like when he smiles. We know this, because while he commu-nicates with his carers through gestures like smiling, he cannot recog-nise himself in a mirror. He spontaneously expresses himself, and this expression takes the form of a smile. This is what Merleau-Ponty meant when he declared that intention and behaviour are internally related. One does not cause the other. Instead they are part of the same configuration and cannot be separated. Of course, adults can manage their self-presentation, deliberately not showing pleasure or displeasure. But the infant is without guile and directly communicates himself to others. But how does he 'know' that the adult with whom he is in communication is expressing a similar intentional state that he then mirrors? How can he infer the adult's state of mind if not through analogy with his own? Here psychologists talk about smiling being a reflex, or 'hard-wired'. But this does not explain what is going on here; it simply explains it away. Once biology is called on like this, psychologists assume it isn't their business, and that neurologists or evolutionary biology will have the explanation at a different level of organisation. Both Mead and Merleau-Ponty insist that this reduc-tionist sort of explanation just will not do. Phenomena belonging to the human order, like smiling, cannot be explained through appeal at the lower court of the vital order. Of course people are animals, but everything in us is personal and cultural as well as natural. So the cultural and natural cannot ever be separated out, and certainly the former cannot be reduced to the latter. Instead, the partaking in a higher human order transforms events in the natural order. The fact that smiling *means* something to people changes how we analyse it – it can never be understood in terms of nerves and muscle twitches.

To understand this 'smiling reflex', we have to escape our natural attitude of dualism, difficult though this might be. We have to get away from cognitions inside bodies, as well as from baby variables and situation variables. We need to think laterally, employ an alternative construction that makes sense of the phenomenon. Merleau-Ponty suggests that one of the important properties of the human body-subject is that it reads other people's intentions directly and pre-reflectively; knows what they mean without having to infer it from their behaviour. Of course, we can get other people's intentions wrong, they might deceive us, for example. So here 'knowing' doesn't imply that we always get things right. But we do not have to go through a process of deliberation or reasoning to arrive at an understanding of other people. We know other people by how they conduct themselves. Their intentionality is not an internal mental state, but turned outwards onto the world that we share with them. In other words, when we see someone smile at us, we do not go through a long and complicated set of cognitive processes to arrive at a conclusion about how it is to be interpreted. This may be how a computer would approach things, but we are not computers. Instead, we perceive the smile as friendly or false immediately and act accordingly. The whole perception is greater than the sum of the parts (for example putting together information about the position of the mouth, the configuration around the eyes and the general tension of the body) that make it up. Merleau-Ponty (1962, 1964) makes this case by referring to infant studies, arguing that body-subjects naturally assume an identity between things as they are and things as they appear:

> The child lives in a world which he unhesitatingly believes accessible to all around him. He has no awareness of himself or of others as private subjectivities, nor does he suspect that all of us, himself included, are limited to one certain point of view of the world ... He has no knowledge of points of view. For him, men are empty heads turned towards one single, self-evident world. (Merleau-Ponty, 1962: 355)

Merleau-Ponty (1964) also mentions the object relations theory of Melanie Klein. In her observation and psychoanalysis of children, she had stressed the importance of projective identification (see Chapter 3). This is the process whereby the infant projects his feelings into his mother, resulting in her experiencing the baby's distress or contentment. Any parent will recognise this. When your baby is desperately upset, it is as though you, the parent, experience his distress at first hand. You feel upset and have to do something to relieve it.

The Kleinians (Anderson, 1992) proposed that the parent's job is to contain the upset. This involves unconsciously transmitting the message back to the baby that although he feels desperate now, it will all be all right soon; there's nothing to fret about. This is not a denial of his feeling, but an attempt to hold and contain his wildest panic.

Both Merleau-Ponty and Klein see this pre-reflective interaction as the basis of what we think of as empathy in the human order. It is the ground on which our understanding of others is based. For the human body-subject, life begins in synchrony with significant others. We do not start out as separate individuals each with his internalised self and personality. We are part of other people – in internal relations with them. Our individuality is an achievement and a construction, not a given. However, there is always separateness, a sense of the other person as other. What we see is the way other people comport themselves. It is through this intersubjectivity, the way in which we are all of us in the world, that we understand them. We never literally feel their pain:

> The grief and the anger of another have never quite the same significance for him as they have for me. For him these situations are lived through, for me they are displayed. (Merleau-Ponty, 1962: 356)

The other does then require reading or interpretation. Hermeneutic interpretation requires that something is different enough to require interpreting, but similar enough to be understood. Understanding rests on a similar grounding without which it is impossible. We will never be able to understand a cat, a dog or a Martian in the same way that we do another person. They are just too different from us and we have difficulty in putting ourselves in their positions. What Merleau-Ponty emphasised was this similar grounding in human embodiment. From this perspective, many of the phenomena identified by cognitive social psychology like group contagion and the fundamental attribution error are not so puzzling (Langdridge and Butt, in press). They represent our reversion to a primitive way of relating. They may be problematic, as when people were caught up in Nazi ideology, but they are not a mystery. For good or ill, we are inextricably intertwined with other people. This is what it means to be in the human order. The sociality that both Mead and Kelly prized is at the centre of the human project. Mead theorised the self-process, seeing it as emerging from the conversation of gestures with significant others. Kelly's position on sociality is more ambiguous and needs some elaboration.

Dennis Hinkle, one of Kelly's students, quoted Kelly as saying that his 'sociality corollary' was in many ways the main issue for him in the psychology of personal constructs (Hinkle, 1970). This corollary is the one that differentiates two ways of acting towards people: as 'behaving mannequins' or as construers like ourselves. Kelly derided reacting to people as mannequins as essentially psychopathic, treating other people in terms of what they will do to or for us. For him, playing a role (that is, construing the construction processes of the other and acting in the light of that) was the moral way to behave. In his view it was also the only effective way to bring about personal change. The therapist has to see things from the clients' point of view first. This does not mean agreeing with them, but appreciating their perspective; knowing 'where they're coming from'. This is what understanding means and shows the phenomenological influence in Kelly. Understanding does not mean agreeing with or excusing, but recognising a different world view. Construing the construction processes of the other can be read as thinking our way into the other person's shoes in a deliberate and thought-out way. And sometimes we do this. When I am trying to think what to buy someone as a present, I try to imagine what he'd like and what use he would make of a particular gift. But often, this construing process takes place at a more tacit level. So in a game of tennis, we might anticipate the other's shot and are able to volley successfully because we do. But here, there is literally no time to think; we read the other person and move to anticipate him before we could say what we have done or indeed how we did it (Butt, 1998).

The problem is that if we take all sociality to be based on the paradigm of deliberate thought, we come to see thought, like construing, as something that precedes behaviour. It appears to be behind it, powering it. This in turn leads to us reifying constructs, thinking of them as entities inside the person to be extracted with a repertory grid. We lose the phenomenological reading of PCT when we think of constructs rather than construing; of cognitive entities rather than a process. And this is the reading that is taken up by Mischel when he considers what construing means. In the cognitive social approach, construing is a form of thinking. But construing does not take place behind action, but in the action itself. Action, thought and affect are internally related and not separate provinces of the mind. This is why, in his fundamental postulate, Kelly writes of 'a person's processes' and not of the way a person thinks, feels and acts. We can do things deliberately and with effort we might cognitively control our emotions. But this is the exception and not the rule. In the normal course of events, we act pre-reflectively. We simply do not have time to think about everything we do or say, yet what we say and do seems to carry our intentions rather well. In fact, what we say and do often seems to firm up our thoughts and intentions. We find ourselves in our words and deeds. This is what Merleau-Ponty meant when he said that language was 'not the clothing of thought', or 'the expression of . . . a meaning already clear to itself' (1962: 388). Our social acts cannot be thought of as expressions or consequences of ready-made thought and intention. Neither can they be seen as any individual's exclusive property. The internal relationship between each of us and other actors means that we change our action as they do. We will now consider this joint action in more detail.

Joint action

There is undoubtedly a paradox surrounding the way our personality appears to us in different situations. On the one hand, we feel like the same person wherever we are. We have no difficulty in recognising a thread that runs though time and place, identifying us as the people we are. We retain a sense of self, recognising the same person in the distant past as the one we are today. But on the other hand, we feel almost like different people in the lecture theatre, the pub, with our parents or our best friend. We find ourselves supporting one set of arguments with our friends, and championing a completely different point of view with our mum and dad. We are the life and soul of the party but overserious with our partner. And none of this feels like acting to us. It appears to us that we are acting quite naturally when we apparently contradict ourselves or act like a completely different person in two different social contexts. Mischel (1968) did a great service to personality theory when he forced this issue to the fore, exposing the theoretical bankruptcy of trait theory. But his solution, as we have seen above, is framed in terms of objective thought. A phenomenological analysis of this issue begins with Mead's conception of the social act.

Mead (1982a), it will be remembered, contended that the success of the human species was due to their cooperation in the face of adversity. We have evolved the ability to read and anticipate each other, through gestures and later language. Each participant in a social act does not know where it is leading because, as it were, they think on their feet. We constantly adjust and modify our conduct in the light of how we think it is being construed by the other(s). What might start off as good-natured joshing might end up as an ill-tempered argument, while what was meant to be just a friendly chat leads to a sexual embrace. On rare occasions, one person might deviously and cleverly manipulate the other, managing impressions and subtly influencing where an encounter is going. It is a salesperson's job to get you to buy something even though you never intended to walk out of the shop or showroom having rushed your decision. But such encounters are the exceptions that illustrate the rule. We pick out such instances precisely because they are exceptional and usually break an unwritten rule. Normally, we interact pre-reflectively with other people. What makes social life interesting and valuable is that the whole interaction cannot be simply assembled from the parts. It is the organising of the parts into a meaningful gestalt that characterises interactions in the human order.

It is this formulation of the social act that Blumer (1969) and Shotter (1993) refer to as 'joint action'. The outcome of a social act cannot be traced back to the individual intentions of any of the participants. Shotter (1993) distinguishes three types of knowledge: knowing that (in the way that we know facts or information), knowing how (as when we know how to perform a skilled activity) and knowing from within a social situation. It is this last kind that characterises joint action. Here, two (or more) people are in a dialectical relationship. What goes on within them is not prior to what goes on between them. What goes on within each – in terms of thoughts and actions – unfolds in the light of the relationship between them. We cannot separate the dyad into its constituent parts (person and situation variables) and retain the meaning of the interaction. There is not a sequence in which you act, I perceive, I reflect, I act and then you perceive and so on. As Kelly was fond of saying, we live in anticipation. We construe in action, not before it. So often we find ourselves acting in a way that we could not predict because we are taken over by joint action. Shotter underlines that one of its properties is that it feels given, or outside us. This is when we are likely to disavow responsibility and see it as residing in the situation. Recently I had a vivid example of this in my own life. I met up with four people with whom I had shared a student house thirty years ago. We had not met since as a group, although one or two people had kept in distant contact with each other. With the only history we shared being thirty years previously, it was astonishing how quickly we reverted to the roles we once played with each other. Being a professor, a teacher or a TV presenter played no part in our reunion. Our current selves were bracketed off as we reverted to long-lost patterns of interaction. Nobody planned that this would happen and everybody was surprised by the extent of it.

Conversation is a particularly good example of joint action. In everyday situations, we do not think before we speak. And yet, what we say conveys what we want to express pre-reflectively. It usually makes good sense to us; we don't have to endlessly correct ourselves and deliberate on our speech. If we do, our reflective self-consciousness usually interferes with our expression. The observation that we can talk sensibly without deliberately thinking shows very neatly how the natural attitude of objective thought and dualism misrepresent what Merleau-Ponty refers to as the 'lived world'; things as we actually experience them:

> In the experience of dialogue, there is constituted between the other person and myself a common ground; my thought and his are inter-woven into a single fabric, my words and those of my interlocutor are called forth by the state of the discussion, and they are inserted into a shared operation of which neither of us is the creator ... In the present dialogue, I am freed from myself, for the other person's thoughts are certainly his; they are not of my making, though I do grasp them the moment they come into being, or even anticipate them. And indeed, the objections which my interlocutor raises to what I say draws from me thoughts which I had no idea I possessed, so that at the same time I lend him my thoughts, he reciprocates by making me think too. (Merleau-Ponty, 1962: 354)

This passage clearly highlights the paradox that we experience in joint action. On the one hand, 'the other person's thoughts are certainly his'; there is indeed a private realm that we may code as the self, even though it is the product of our participation in the public realm. But also the other person 'draws from me thoughts which I had no idea I possessed'. The social act draws us out and extends us – we create as well as discover ourselves in joint action. This is a very different conception from the one in personality theory that attempts to divide the field up into person and situation variables that come together in a complex interaction that produces behaviour. In joint action, the whole interaction is greater than the sum of the parts. Social acts conjure up selves that outrun us. Think about the difficulties that we have with others – whether with friends, partners, parents or children. Trying to freeze this in terms of variables, essentially whose fault it is, does not capture the dynamic of the relations involves. We are forever anticipating and at the same time unaware of our anticipations and how they influence the other. The person and the situation therefore cannot be separated and causal relations allotted to either.

Nonetheless, each person develops both his own particular existential project in the world, as well as a sense of self that reflects this project to a greater or lesser degree. For Merleau-Ponty (1962), a person's project comprised a set of pre-reflective engagements that come to embody his chosen way of being-in-the-world. He uses the term 'sedimented' to capture the way in which this project is carried into habitual behaviours or actions that do not necessarily feel freely chosen by the person. A person's sense of self reflects his sense of integrity that transcends time and situation, but may not accurately reflect the full extent of one's existential project. This notion of project will be an important feature of the last chapters. In the next chapter, I will consider the sense of self.

7

The Sense of Self

The self is a fuzzy concept. In sociological and social psychological literature, terms like 'self', 'identity' and 'subjectivity' are often used loosely, although these different terms have arisen in different theoretical frameworks (Elliott, 2001). Harré (1989) points out that the concept of self is fraught with grammatical confusion. Nevertheless, as we saw in Chapter 3, some humanists (for example Rogers) place the self at the centre of their understanding of personality, and this formulation is one commonly taken up in everyday folk psychology. The self is an internal and creative gyroscope, forever directing us, demanding expression and pushing towards actualisation. Thwarting of the self is at the heart of neurosis. We can think of this as the doctrine of the essential self; the proposition that each person has at her centre an essential core that is present at birth. At the other end of the personality spectrum, the social constructionists, as well as radical behaviourists like Skinner (1974), regard the self as an explanatory fiction. It is a modernist myth that serves to bestow an illusory individual agency and distracts our attention away from the discourses that create it. This dichotomy in many ways mirrors the agency/structure debate in sociology (Walsh, 1998; Archer, 2000). Although this issue is new in psychology, sociologists have debated the relative importance of individual agency and social structure throughout the twentieth century. Are individuals merely puppets whose strings are pulled by the ideological forces (or surrounding discourses) in society? As we have seen, Berger and Luckmann's (1967) project was aimed precisely at overcoming this agency/structure issue. Their dialectic, it will be remembered, sees the self as a social construction, but nevertheless a centre for a degree of agency once constructed. This is not a pre-existing essential self that enjoys total agency and control. Berger and Luckmann (1967) drew on Mead's concept of sociality to theorise a decentred self that, to paraphrase Marx, makes history, but not in circumstances of its own making.

In this chapter, I want to develop an understanding of self-phenomena that both takes our experience of self seriously and, at the same time, recognises the importance of social context and joint action. I will argue that while the self has assumed a new importance in late modernity, it cannot be dismissed as a modern creation; the programming of the docile body with the software of disciplinary control. I will begin by tracing the development of the self in the context of modernity. Here, we will be able to appreciate the increasing salience of the self in our modern social world. I will then outline the features of what I will call the 'existential self'. This is shorthand for the self-experience of the body-subject that has been elaborated in both existential phenomenology and pragmatism. Finally, I will look at the issues of the self that personality theorists focus upon: the sense of fragmentation and integrity of the self-concept, and an understanding of personal agency and choice.

The self in late modernity

In order to understand the importance of the self to us in today's society, it will be useful to try to stand back from the natural attitude that envelops us. Phenomenological seeing, it will be remembered, involves trying to free ourselves from preconceptions and appreciating alternative constructions. It is all too easy to think of ourselves as selves inhabiting bodies, and this is why folk psychology draws so heavily on the humanism of Rogers. Inside each body, a self is buried, craving expression and demanding actualisation. Since we cannot always do or say exactly what we want to, we think of society as a hindrance that stands in the way of our natural self-expression. Often we don't know precisely what we want, but we are sure that it isn't what we're getting, and it's easy to think that we have been suppressed and diverted in some important way by extraneous impediments. It is also easy to focus on others and imagine that their lot is better than ours. So we are very ready to accept the dualistic and individualistic formulation of Rogers' humanism. Liberation seems to be based on the freeing of some internal self-impulse from the restraints of society.

But let's think not of selves inside bodies, but of body-subjects. From our earliest interactions, we are intimately aware of our relationships with significant others and their reactions to us. Every body-subject has the power of agency; we exert a degree of control over our physical environment as we move our bodies and the things within our reach. We are not simply the 'docile bodies' that Foucault (1977) claimed, that are inscribed with disciplinary power. A degree of power goes with the territory of being a body-subject; the person is a form of motion. As we adjust our actions and impulses in social acts with others, and as we silently anticipate their construing of us, we become increasingly aware of ourselves both as agents and as objects in the eyes of others. This leads to the distinction between *I* and *me* that Mead underlined. What is cultural and what is natural are inextricably mixed and virtually impossible to separate out. Reflection occasioned by social interaction is an essential aspect of social life and the pre-reflective and reflective phases of our action become fused into our personalities.

Giddens (1991) argues that in late modern societies, this reflective phase has become enormously more important. This has led to a culture in which the self has become emphasised, and what he terms 'expert systems' like psychotherapy have flourished to service the self. What Giddens calls the 'reflexive project of self' is at the centre of late modern life. This is because the change from traditional to modern society disembedded individuals from a traditional inflexible social order. 'Disembedding' is a very apt metaphor here. Giddens, a sociologist, sees the person as very much a social construction; a product of the society that surrounds her. What is special about late modern society, he argues, is that it digs people out of their social moorings in traditional families. In traditional societies, most people lived and died not far from where they were born. Before the Industrial Revolution, they worked where they lived and encountered the same people all the time in their everyday lives. 'Going to work' is a concept familiar to us, but nevertheless one that would be strange to people living in traditional societies. When we conceptualise the self as a product of social interaction, we can see that very different selves might be produced at work, at leisure and with one's family. What constitutes one's true self is simply not an issue that would arise outside the late modern social context.

For Giddens (1991), the reflexive project of self is a central feature of late modernity. The individual is disembedded from the moorings characteristic in traditional societies, and is faced with choices about who to be and what to become. Gone are the restricting certainties of traditional society where action is inextricably tied in to social position. In late modern society, the individual is faced with a kaleidoscope of possibilities and choices, which present both threats and opportunities. This necessitates an increasing use of reflection, in which individuals look critically at their action and ask what they are making of themselves. Social action is carried out and even sometimes planned in the knowledge that they are deciding on more than the action per se but on the projects of self and identity. Each act now potentially defines us; what we are doing indicates who we are. It is therefore necessary for individuals in late modernity constantly to monitor their action, reflect on their thoughts and feelings and manage their trajectory of self. Individuals have taken charge of their lives, with all the consequences of risk and excitement that this entails. The things we do in our leisure time, what we eat and the hobbies we pursue are all evidence to both others and ourselves of what sort of person we take ourselves to be. In traditional societies, even the way people dressed was not a matter of choice, but a clear indication of social status. Now, we are faced with a vast number of ways of expressing ourselves, and the way we dress is a signal to others of the way we would like to be taken.

Nowhere is this reflexive project more salient than in our relations with others. In traditional societies, relationships were dictated by the social order in such a way as to relieve individuals of responsibility for the way that they conducted themselves with others. Late modernity has seen the invention of what Giddens calls the 'pure relationship'. This is not to be confused with a sexual relationship. Indeed, the paradigm case seems to be the friendship; a relationship entered into on the basis of mutual affection:

> The pure relationship is one in which external criteria have become dissolved: the relationship exists solely for whatever rewards the relationship as such can deliver. (Giddens, 1991: 6)

In traditional societies, relationships were means to the end of mere survival. People were bound by reciprocal sets of obligation, which guaranteed the survival of the group. Now these means have become ends in themselves. Freed from traditional ties, individuals now focus on and manage their interactions in a manner hitherto impossible. Giddens (1991) reminds us that our relationships with our marriage partners, our children and our concept of friendship all differ dramatically from those available to pre-modern Europeans.

But the plurality of choice thrown up produces threats as well as opportunities. Giddens argues that the practice of psychotherapy and counselling is just one example of an expert system that has grown as a result of this transformation of intimacy. Although therapy is saturated with the vocabulary of pathology and neurosis, the ever-increasing demand for it in contemporary society is partly explained in terms of its power to help individuals to reflect on and plan their lifestyle. The ready assimilation of Rogers' humanism into folk psychology makes sense when we understand the reflexive project of self that is at the heart of late modern times. Although personal agency (Mead's *I*) has always been a property of body-subjects, the *me* is increasingly important in today's social world.

The existential self

So the self has assumed a more definite profile in late modernity. However, this does not mean that it is a discursive production. Foucault's claim that the self has been conjured into existence through the discourses of disciplinary power does not follow necessarily from the observation that the reflexive self-project is a vital feature of our times. There is no doubt that the social constructionist attack on the self, based as it is on Foucault's analysis, is a valuable counterweight to humanistic psychology's view that the self is semi-detached from the person; an internal substance that is separate from and owner of the body. Social constructionism's critique is aimed at this Cartesian self (Bakhurst and Sypnowich, 1995) and shares much with the existentialist and pragmatist positions. Both identify the self with the body (as do radical behaviourists and social learning theorists – see Mischel and Mischel, 1977 and Day, 1977). Both see the self as a social product, something that is produced in interactions with other people. But for both Mead and Merleau-Ponty, some form of self-process is an inevitable consequence of partaking of the human order (Mead, 1982a, 1982b; Merleau-Ponty, 1963; Rosenthal and Bourgeois, 1991). Body-subjects develop knowledge of themselves and others simultaneously, taking the perspectives of others in a way that produces self-reflection. The self is therefore not a central essence of each person, but a process that has its roots in social interaction.

Bakhurst and Sypnowich (1995) argue that perhaps the main reason for the appeal of the humanistic self is that it appears to preserve each person's sense of identity and uniqueness. Modern psychology no longer seriously subscribes to a simple Cartesian doctrine in which the self is like a soul; a different substance from the body. But we are loath to give up the idea that we are unique individuals, each with our own set of thoughts, fantasies and feelings. Each of us knows that we are both similar to and at the same time different from others. The concept of the self seems to offer a piece of Cartesian wreckage onto which we may cling in order to proclaim the personal nature of our constructions. The existentialist self offers a way of both under-standing the social origins of the self and appreciating the particular perspective of each individual person. It is neither a Cartesian ghost nor a discursive mirage. To 'have a self' means to be able to reflect on our action and appearance from another perspective. This may be from the viewpoint of a specific or a generalised other. To think and reflect we have to use inner dialogue, a public language imported into our private sphere. But it is undeniable that everyone has a sense of self. It feels to them as if they have some core, some unique property, a signature that marks them out as an individual. Under-standing people involves taking account of *both* their experience *and* the social context in which it arises.

One of the ways in which phenomenologists investigate experience is through a technique called 'imaginative variation' (Ihde, 1986). This is a version of thought experiment in which we vary things in our imagination in order to clarify the meaning. It is useful to apply this to what we mean by a sense of self. What would have to change so that we no longer had a sense of self? Suppose you woke up one morn-ing and had no memory of anything at all. You didn't know your name, where you lived, who your friends were or if you had a partner. You found that when you got in a car (you didn't know if it was yours or not), you could drive it without thinking about it. Seated at a piano, you found that you were quite an accomplished pianist. How would this type of memory loss affect your sense of self? I think it would be greatly affected. You might say to yourself 'I'm a car-driver and a piano-player', but this would not really constitute much of an identity. There is a great difference between being able to do something and basing an identity and a sense of self on it. Similarly, if you were unable to project yourself into the future, make plans and anticipate things, your sense of self would be lost or at least greatly impoverished. This was the position of Schneider, the brain-damaged patient who Merleau-Ponty used as an example through-out his *Phenomenology of Perception* (1962). Schneider certainly had a pre-reflective connection with his world that enabled him to draw on reflexes (like scratching an itch) and on skills learned. But he had lost his connection with the human order, the ability to project himself into the past or future using abstract thought. In effect, he was what Foucault seems to suggest a person in pre-modern society would be like – a docile body without the imprint of disciplinary power. But this is surely nonsense. Schneider had lost more than modern society – he had lost the human order.

Keen (1975) argues that it is the way that we body-subjects inhabit time that makes us into selves. Clearly, both the past and the future influence my cat. When I move to the cupboard and take out a tin of cat food, she prepares herself for feeding. A sequence of events has been learned that leads to a smooth behavioural pattern. The early behaviourists tried to make this conditioning a paradigm of human action. As Merleau-Ponty (1963) pointed out, some type of adaptation is a feature of the vital order. We might account for Schneider's habits in terms of conditioning. But as the evidence amassed by the social learning theorists demonstrated, what was usually thought of as human conditioning was mediated by some form of awareness (Bandura, 1969). We inhabit time in a different way from cats, projecting ourselves into different possible futures and deliberating whether to do one thing or another. When I am deciding whether to carry on working, watch TV or go to the pub, I engage in an internal dialogue that is based on the dialogues I have seen and taken part in the public sphere. Deliberation before action requires my immersion in the symbolic universe of the human order. When my cat sees me reach for the cat food, she can't say to herself 'Here he is, man the tin-opener' because she doesn't have the power of speech (I do occasionally think she's going to say something, probably quite contemptuous, about the food but nothing yet!).

We are time-beings in a very special way. Human time is very different from the time envisaged in objective thought. It does not proceed in a simple linear fashion, but has all the ambiguity of the lived world. Things that happened last year seem curiously very recent and at the same time an age ago. Memories can be at the same time sweet and painful and anticipations exciting and full of foreboding. When we remember and anticipate, we appropriate the past and future into our present. If I tell you about my earliest memory, it tells you nothing about what happened to me back then. It tells you about me *now*, indicating the sense I make of things and the stories I tell myself. Neither you nor I can know how accurate my memory is. But from a phenomenological perspective, this doesn't matter. The memory speaks of the way the world is experienced rather than of any objective truth. And understanding me involves appreciating the way I see and feel things, not knowing what 'really' happened.

Similarly, when I am excited on my way to the airport to meet an old friend, the future I am living in might bear little resemblance to what eventually happens. Our joint action and the situation in which we find ourselves might be different from what I imagine. But we live in anticipation. It shows in our posture, gestures and feelings – our whole stance and attitude towards the world. What makes us human, and at the same time different from each other, is our different anticipatory stances, the way in which we experience the future. As Keen (1975) argues, this is what it means to have a sense of self. It is this way of living in time that gives us a sense of integrity and continuation.

In many ways, Kelly's concept of 'core role structure' captures the essential features of the existentialist self. The metaphor of core is important. It implies that there is something vital at the centre of the person, different from but an integral part of the flesh that surrounds it. Nonetheless, this core is a construction. It is something that is built up through experience in the world. It does not predate construing and does not cause or direct behaviour. Kelly was explicit in his rejection of Cartesian dualism. His concept of role is also important here. It reproduces Mead's concept of sociality, emphasising that we interact with other people through construing and anticipating their constructions. 'Core role' therefore emphasises that at the heart of the person's experience is something that feels essentially like a true self, an essence. Nevertheless, this core is a social construction, something that arises in and through contact with others. The self is therefore multifaceted, not unitary. Kelly argued that what constitutes consistency in behaviour cannot be objectively defined. What is important is the sense that the actor herself makes of her own action. Nonetheless, none of us lives in a social vacuum and it is not only us but others who have to make sense of our action. Through taking the perspective of others, each actor will get the message about whether they are presenting a socially coherent self to others.

Fragmentation and the sense of self

The construction of a coherent self is particularly problematic when we distribute our interactions across a wide range of different social situations. When we live and work in the same places and among the same people, 'being oneself' would not be an issue. It is only when we move out of traditional communities in the modern world, donning different roles and feeling inconsistent with ourselves in these different roles that the issue arises. More work has to be done to present ourselves as unified people. While social learning theorists like Mischel (1968) saw this in terms of situation-specificity, the problem has not been ignored in the humanist camp. Mair's (1977) metaphor of the community of self and Rowan's (1990) work on 'sub-personalities' are just two examples of the way in which the plurality of personality has been theorised. The fact is that however convincing the arguments about the primacy of situation, role and discourse in the influencing of action, each of us does carry a sense of self and feels discomfort when this is in some way fragmented. What accounts for this experience?

In the last chapter, I emphasised the importance of joint action. In our social interactions, we find ourselves in engagements that outrun us. Our individual agency is subordinated to joint projects as we lend ourselves to the social contexts in which we find ourselves. We appear to conjure up different selves in different situations. Nonetheless, we each have a sense of self. We experience ourselves as having a thread that runs though time and space. Indeed, we might think of having a self as meaning that I recognise myself in the past and can project myself into imaginary futures (Keen, 1975). I look at a photograph of myself as a child and unhesitatingly identify it as me. The things I said and did when I'd had a few drinks cannot be disowned entirely and laid at the door of the alcohol and the situation. The embarrassment I experience testifies to my intentionality that was let loose and facilitated by these 'situational variables'. So how are we to understand this sense of self and its relation to our actions and interactions? Butt et al. (1997a) carried out an investigation into people's sense of fragmentation and their sense of self. Before describing this study, it is important to say something about grid method generally and its relation to phenomenology.

Grid methodology is a flexible method designed by Kelly (1955) to investigate personality. The columns in the grid are elements that are subject to the constructs that make up the grid's rows (see Fransella and Bannister, 1977). In the classical repertory grid devised by Kelly (1955), the elements are people known to the participant, who then construes them in terms of elicited constructs. So Chris might consider the elements, me, mum and dad, and say that while mum and me are both considerate, dad is irritable. Considerate–irritable is then a bipolar construct through which all the elements are then construed, say, on a seven-point rating scale. Correlation coefficients between constructs (and elements) may then be used to indicate, if only tentatively, the structure of a person's construct system. It is important to note two points. Firstly, the aim is not to find out what

Chris, mum and dad are 'really like', or which traits they possess. We are only interested in the way things appear to Chris. Secondly, a bipolar construct does not comprise logical opposites. 'Considerate' and 'irritable' are not logical opposites. The world is not divided into people who have one attribute and not the other. But the point is that in the eyes of this participant, it is a meaningful distinction. The investigator must adopt what Kelly (1955) calls a 'credulous approach', trying to capture the way things appear to the participant, while at the same time maintaining a critical distance from it. This is crucial in psychotherapy and also in phenomenological interviewing (Moustakas, 1994). Of course, it may be that not all the elements fall within what Kelly called the 'range of convenience' of a particular construct. Some people may be seen as neither considerate nor irritable. It is not that they are in between the two, but just not in range of the construct. While Chris may think of those she lives with in these terms, they might simply not be relevant when she considers a shopkeeper, or a film star she admires. Again, the aim of the grid is to get to the way things appear to Chris without forcing her constructions into a logical straitjacket.

Grid method is ideal for helping people to think about and reflect on the way things appear to them. Like orthodox phenomenological methods, it focuses closely on particular cases (elements) to help people to grasp the way things appear (constructs). It deviates from phenomenology when the structure of a construct system is thought to be revealed through correlation. Here it moves away from the way things appear to being theory-driven in a way that would be rejected by phenomenologists. Phenomenologists also reject the presupposition of a general bipolar structure of meaning. All the same, the relationship between constructs as indicated by a grid may be incorporated into an interview so as to help people to reflect on an aspect of their lives. From a phenomenological point of view, it is important to think of the grid-interview as a process that helps people to reflect. It is not a way of discovering an underlying cognitive structure. Butt et al. (1997a) used this approach in their study. They interviewed eleven participants using a novel form of grid-interview in an effort to get people to reflect on themselves in joint action. The elements of the grid were not people, but aspects of the participants' own self. Participants were asked to think initially about the full range of their social behaviour, how differently they conducted themselves with different other people. They then wrote 'me when I'm with x, y and z' (different people) on separate index cards. They were then asked to consider these cards in pairs, focusing on how they acted differently with, say, x and y. So the constructs in the grid were these differences in action (for example 'I laugh and joke with Nick, but am careful what I say with Matt'). Once pairs of card had been used to elicit what the participant felt was a full range of their social action, the grid was used to get them to consider each of the elements in the light of each construct. They filled in the grid, marking who they laughed and joked with (1), who they were careful with (0) and who was outside the range of the construct (×).

The participants were then asked to look at the grid and think further about patterns of interaction that occurred to them. It was interesting that all but one of them spontaneously employed a construct labelled something like 'feel or be myself' versus ' don't feel/ unable to be myself'. And in the interviews, the interviewers drew participants' attention to this issue, asking them to think about what it meant to be oneself. What was significant was that while all participants had a sense of what it was to 'be themselves', this was not in any way related to their exhibiting particular traits or behaviours. Ken's grid, shown in Table 7.1, is a good example of this.

Table 7.1   Ken's grid

Me with . . .

1	Dad	Alan	Cleo	Fred	Jim	Roy	Paul	Dan	0
Connect with	1	1	1	×	0	0	1	0	Don't care
Defer to	1	×	0	×	0	1	0	×	Dominate
Patient	1	0	0	0	0	×	1	0	Not patient
Passionate	1	1	1	1	×	0	1	0	Instrumental
Laugh	×	0	1	×	×	0	1	0	Serious
Protective	0	×	1	×	×	×	1	×	Protected
Responsible	0	×	1	×	0	×	1	0	Free
Control me	1	×	1	×	0	1	×	0	Control them
Look up to	1	×	1	0	0	0	1	0	Don't look up to
Inspirational	1	1	×	0	0	0	1	0	Confirmatory
Real self	1	×	1	×	×	0	×	0	Acting

Source: Butt et al. 1997a

Ken only felt that he was himself in the presence of two people: his dad and Cleo (his partner). Yet how he acted with them was quite different. In fact, he found himself acting in opposite ways with these two central people. Looking at this grid, we can readily appreciate Mischel's point that trait descriptions do not capture the essence of a person. So what do people mean by 'being themselves'? When considering this, participants repeatedly mentioned the absence of self-consciousness and self-monitoring. Being yourself meant not having to watch yourself and allowing your behaviour to flow naturally in the situation. It meant lending yourself to joint action; taking part in social acts without having to worry about it. Paradoxically, being oneself does not mean being consistent across situations, but quite the reverse; it means relaxing into social life and not having to worry about the managing of impressions. Being a person means being involved in social interaction – being-in-the-world. This is how we extend ourselves, both finding and constructing ourselves in interactions with others. George Kelly summed this up very nicely in a critique of Cartesian dualism:

> A good deal is said these days about being oneself. It is supposed to be healthy to be oneself. While it is a little hard for me to understand how one could be anything else, I suppose what is meant is that one should not strive to become anything other than what one is. This strikes me as a very dull way of living; in fact I would be inclined to argue that all of us would be better off if we set out to become other than what we are. Well, I'm not sure we would be *better* off – perhaps it would be more accurate to say life would be a lot more *interesting*. (Kelly, 1969f: 157)

Here, of course, Kelly was referring to 'being oneself' in the Rogerian sense. The psychology of personal constructs is built on a conception of agency that underlines that we set out on a course of action never knowing exactly where it will lead us. We can attempt to construe the other's constructions and reflect upon what we are doing, but we can never be certain how things will turn out because other people are agents too, and our interweaving with them confers both uncertainty and excitement to our behavioural projects. But this is what life is about. This brings us to a discussion of personal agency.

Personal agency

Although we are all carried along in the flow of joint action, this does not mean that individual people are always without a degree of personal agency. Our connection with others is primarily pre-reflective. We do not have to think about how the interaction is going and, indeed, feel comfortable to be ourselves when we are moving effortlessly in a dance with others. We are most comfortable when we can just flow along with other people in joint action. Nevertheless, we can reflect and deliberate on our action. If it seems vital to us to make a good impression, we can and do try to manage interactions so as to be seen in the best possible light. Sadly, it is often the case that this is when we are often not at our best, as self-consciousness stiffens our performance! Our plans frequently do not lead us where we had hoped, but we certainly do plan and direct our action. Personality theorists (Baumeister, 1999; Pervin and John, 2001) draw on a concept of self to explain this deliberate and integrative aspect of people's behaviour.

As I argued above (following Keen, 1975), what 'having a self' means is having a constructive relationship to the past and the future. It is not that past events cause anything in our action, but the way in which we make sense of them clearly informs everything we do. Similarly, nothing in the future can determine what we do. Nevertheless, we live in anticipation, and the stance we take towards things inevitably affects how we act as well as how others act in relation to us. Suppose you are due to meet up with Alison, an old friend, and you are expecting her to criticise you. Perhaps you think that she didn't like the way you acted the last time you met. You were vaguely conscious of a coolness in her manner and a lack of the easy-going conversation that normally characterised your meetings. You don't know exactly what was wrong, but since you last met her, you have mulled over things in a series of inner conversations. In these silent internalised dialogues, you have felt increasingly indignant at being misjudged, first justifying yourself, and later feeling annoyed at having to do so. Now, it may be that you have picked up something about her feelings towards you, but it also may be that you are on the wrong track completely. All the same, you have ended up feeling wrong-footed, somewhat indignant and defensive. It is highly likely that when you eventually meet, your feelings will be evident in your posture and gestures, even if you manage not to actually say anything to underline your behaviour. There is no telling how the interaction will end up, because, as we have seen, a social act is a joint enterprise and both parties involved in it constantly anticipate and react to what they construe as the other's intentions. Perhaps Alison was back to her old self – chatty and friendly, but you still felt a bit resentful and didn't respond to this. Finally, there was a row about something quite trivial. Afterwards, you may say 'I didn't do anything – it's typical of her, she's just too sensitive'. However, you have contributed a strong input into the joint action, and Alison might say it's all your fault – you always brood over things and are too moody. The traits each of you applies to the other are blunt instruments that attempt to capture patterns of behaviour. They miss the complexity of the joint action, and also the reflective process that provided a strong guide to it.

It is in reflection and silent internal conversation that we often set the course that our social acts take. And it is this private phase of our construing that is thought of as the property of the self. There is nothing wrong with using the term 'self' here as a way of coding this process, but we should note two points about it. Firstly, although reflection is private, in that it cannot be publicly observed, there is nothing mystical about it that requires the conjuring up of Descartes' ghost. When you have an imaginary conversation with Alison, you are essentially importing the public sphere into the private. You can only have the private activity because you have taken part in public social interaction first. You use language, a public tool. And you intentionally relate to other people who populate the social world. What is private is the imagination and abstraction in which we position other people in ways which deny them a contribution of the ability to resist. Even masturbatory fantasies, supposedly the most private of activities, rely on the public social sphere as we imaginatively manipulate other people to act in ways we would like. Secondly, the activities of reflection and deliberation are intimately connected to our (usually pre-reflective) being-in-the-world. This is a dialectical relationship in which there is no simple one-way causal relationship. Instead, each unfolds and develops in the light of the other. In Merleau-Ponty's (1962) terminology, this is an internal relationship, where thought, feeling and action each inform the others and cannot be separated out. Private self-processes must not be ignored, but neither must they be promoted to an unrealistically elevated status.

Having said this, it must be acknowledged that we each have more or less characteristic ways of being-in-the-world that are mirrored and indeed reinforced in private reflection. There are many ways in which our past may appear, many different stories that could be told, a range of alternative constructions that could be applied. As I have emphasised time and again, it is not strictly speaking what happens to us that counts, but the way in which we make sense of it. We may look back sentimentally, thankfully, regretfully, angrily or wistfully. The way we act is always conditioned by the way in which things – the past, other people, the future – appear to us. Our stance in the world affects (but of course, does not determine) the way we are taken by others and speaks of the way the world appears to us. This may well be underlined and reinforced by the self-processes of the private sphere, but once again, there is nothing private about their effects. We can all think of people who, directly we meet them, make us feel depressed or optimistic, careful or carefree, relaxed or excited. Something in their manner, the look in their eyes or the way they move communicates their intentionality, their way of being-in-the-world. This will very rarely be something they are consciously managing. We pick up their pre-reflective engagement and respond to it. This, of course, brings us to the issue of the unconscious and our existential projects, which I will examine in some detail in the next chapter.

8

The Unconscious

In discussing the extent of personal agency at the end of Chapter 7, I raised the issue of unconscious action. It is not at all unusual for us to see people doing something that they appear to be completely unaware of. By this I don't just mean that they might be doing things that are just outside the focus of their consciousness, like twitching or tapping their feet. We always exhibit behaviour that we are not conscious of in this sense. This sort of 'preconscious' behaviour is not controversial (Freud, 1957). But it may be that I think they are purposefully and subtly putting me in a difficult position, irritating me or making me feel guilty. If challenged, they would strenuously deny what I think they're doing, disavowing it as a purposeful action. Now it could be that it's just me who is being oversensitive. Perhaps I often think other people are trying to irritate me or make me feel guilty – it's a characteristic of my construing and not a feature of their personality. There is always a danger of confusing what we read into or project onto other people with what is really their property. And, of course, I am likely to strongly resist the idea that I always see what are really unattractive aspects of me in other people and not myself! Here we see two different examples of what we may term 'unconscious action': either the other person or myself could be deceiving ourselves about what we are in fact doing. Clearly an understanding of people has to deal with such unconscious phenomena. In this chapter, I will outline an understanding of the unconscious from an existential phenomenological perspective. It is important to note here that there is no consensus among existential phenomenologists on the issue of the unconscious. Whereas Sartre (1958) was clearly hostile to psychoanalysis, Merleau-Ponty (1993) in his later writing underlined the convergence between phenomenology and psychoanalysis. However, I will concentrate on the common ground between Sartre and Merleau-Ponty. Both recognised the importance of what are thought of as unconscious phenomena, and both reformulated them, insisting that they can be understood in terms of a fracturing of the person's life-world. As van Deurzen-Smith (1997) argues, existential theorists and therapists would not divide the person into conscious and unconscious realms. As we will see, they find it more useful to think in terms of splits in consciousness and the life-world rather than inventing an unconscious mind with its own laws and logic. Nonetheless, the work of Freud and Klein towers over this theoretical area. So I will begin by underlining the case for the dynamic unconscious that Freud and the psychoanalysts who followed him proposed. Then I will look in some detail at the development of the Freudian concept, before focusing on an existential account.

The dynamic unconscious

Freud's unconscious

It is often wrongly assumed by psychologists that Freud invented the concept of the unconscious. In fact, Romantic poets, philosophers and artists of the nineteenth century had proposed the existence of an unconscious mind that could be accessed through dreams (which Freud referred to as the 'royal road' to the unconscious). Since Descartes' thesis had equated the mind with rational conscious awareness, the existence of an unconscious realm was seen as an explanation of humankind's irrational and emotional aspects. We can see how Freud drew on this distinction where the id, powered by the relentless drive to pleasure, is balanced by the rational ego, with its subordination to the reality principle. Freud's contribution, as Gay (1988) points out, was to argue for (or, in Gay's view, discover) the link between repression and the unconscious. The idea of a dynamic unconscious runs throughout Freud's work, developing from the topographical model, that divided the mind into the unconscious, preconscious and conscious realms, into the structural model, where the id and much of the superego worked at an unconscious level. Freud's model of the unconscious is referred to as 'dynamic' because of the force of repression and the power of unconscious forces to determine conscious activity, albeit in a disguised way. His formal theorising of the concept began in his work on dreams in 1900, and was refined in an essay written in 1915 (Freud, 1953, 1957).

I noted in Chapter 3 how Freud began professional life as a mind–brain identity theorist, seeing mental life as essentially the surface appearance of underlying brain processes. In time, he thought a fully developed psychology would be able to trace its subject matter to brain science, a reductionist faith very much shared by so much of trait theory and cognitive science in present day psychology. Consequently, his theorising was cast in terms of energy transfer and cathexis. Activity began as unconscious but could appear in consciousness (via the preconscious realm; that area of our experience that could potentially be made conscious), provided that energy was available for this transition. However, a psychic censor polices the border of the unconscious and preconscious realms. The function of this censor is to prevent material that is too disturbing to conscious life ever reaching conscious deliberation and consideration. In order to do this, it withdraws the energy necessary for problematic material achieving consciousness. This mechanistic and convoluted explanation was presumably thought necessary for psychoanalysis to be recognised as a scientific pursuit. We are left with the conclusion that the unconscious contains two types of material: that which is yet to be considered by the censor, and that which has been consigned there through the process of repression. It is this latter grouping that constitutes the dynamic unconscious mind and is of interest to psychoanalysis. So the unconscious is not just a dark area that has not been illuminated by the beam of consciousness. It is the repository for unbearable thoughts and images; ideas that would be just too disturbing if they were allowed to see the light of day. In a particularly vivid simile, Gay likens it to a maximum-security prison:

> Most of the unconscious consists of repressed materials. This unconscious, as Freud conceptualised it, is not the segment of mind harbouring thoughts temporarily out of sight and easily recalled; that is what he called the preconscious. Rather, the unconscious proper resembles a maximum-security prison holding anti-social inmates languishing for years or recently arrived, inmates harshly treated and heavily guarded, but barely kept under control and forever attempting to escape. Their breakouts succeed only intermittently, and at great cost to themselves and to others. (Gay, 1988: 128)

The image is a powerful one. Each person is sitting on a powder keg, expending enormous energy keeping ideas at bay that would be just too disturbing even to acknowledge. Nevertheless, the 'breakouts' that Gay mentions occur in dreams all the time. The two mechanisms of sublimation and condensation transform repressed ideas (hence the 'cost to themselves') and allow them some discharge in everyday life. In sublimation, the energy associated with a repressed wish or idea is channelled into other activity. So sexual energy and competitiveness might be channelled into sport, where it can be safely disguised and contained. In condensation, a phenomenon (perhaps an image, a sign or a neurotic symptom) carries the weight of an enormous amount of repressed material. Extending the notion of condensation, Stoller (1986) uses the metaphor of a microdot to make sense of a person's characteristic sexual fantasies. He notes that people carefully craft these fantasies so as to capture as best they can the distilled essence of what is sexually exciting to them. These scenarios are like microdots which, if magnified, reveal the structure of repressed sexual desires long since banished to the unconscious, but allowed expression in condensed form.

It is all too easy to criticise Freudian thinking for its energy-based concepts. But we must bear in mind that he was a man of his time, writing a hundred years ago and trying his best to get psychoanalysis acknowledged as a science. Freudian authorities vary in the extent to which they think he moved away from his mind–brain identity position. Certainly his writing (at least in the English translation) makes the person sound like a mechanism comprising safety valves and pressure gauges. Nevertheless, his mechanistic and neurological speculation was an attempt to understand clinical phenomena. He insisted that repression was a 'finding and not a premise' of psychoanalysis (Freud, 1957: 17). Freud claimed that psychoanalysis was very much a 'bottom-up' rather than a 'top-down' enterprise and seemed proud of his lack of reading in philosophy:

> I have denied myself the very great pleasure of reading Nietzsche, with the deliberate object of not being hampered in working out the impressions received in psycho-analysis by any sort of anticipatory ideas. (1957: 15–16)

Similarly, although he later discovered that the philosopher Schopenhauer had proposed a concept very like repression, Freud claimed that his 'finding' came out of his clinical practice. Repression and the unconscious were concepts with a job to do. They could not be directly observed and were therefore inferred from a person's conduct. But this inference was justified because only with them can we explain the phenomenon of resistance in therapy.

Resistance

Ever since the medical model became the preferred framework for interpreting psychological difficulties in people, these difficulties have been thought of as illnesses. A medical vocabulary has been imported – therapy, treatment, symptoms – that shapes and sometimes restricts our thinking. But one of the ways that so-called 'neurotics' do not fit neatly into the medical model is that they clearly exert some agency and are to some extent the authors of their problems. The anorexic does not eat, the phobic does not confront his fear and the shy person does not risk meeting new people. We can think of ways of construing these issues as along a continuum, with no agency at one end and total agency at the other. If we see them as suffering from some sort of illness or disorder, we accept that they cannot help their plight. The problem here is that some sort of cooperation on the part of clients is essential if they are ever to overcome their problems. If, like Szasz (1970), we see them as responsible agents who are evading their responsibilities, then we would not accept the illness plea, and instead see them as deceiving themselves about their freedom to act. The problem here is that we might easily become involved in victim blaming. Freud's solution was the invention (or discovery?) of the unconscious.

This was a way of reconstruing the agency continuum. Until the turn of the twentieth century, hysterics had been seen as either suffering from a neurological degeneracy (no agency) or moral weakness (total agency). Freud's convoluted theorising was an attempt to explain how and why people acted in self-defeating ways and then resisted attempts to treat their problems. When you go to the doctor with a physical problem, you don't secretly plot to defeat the treatment plan in a variety of subtle ways. But Freud found that this was how his patients' conduct appeared to him. Refusal to remember things, coming late, missing appointments and even introducing techniques of seduction were just some of the strategies that he believed were used to divert successful therapeutic intervention. And it wasn't only psychoanalysts who noted a variety of ways in which sufferers appeared to sabotage therapy and exhibit a resistance to change. Across the therapeutic spectrum, the issue has been reported, albeit in different theoretical frameworks. Berne (1966) noted the 'games' that people indulged in. For example, in 'Why don't you, yes but ...' patients constantly outflank the therapist with reasons why they can't change or do anything differently. In 'If it weren't for you', patients constantly blame someone else, often a partner, who is responsible for spoiling their lives, even when it appears that responsibility may well be shared. Kelly (1955) arrived at the concept of 'core construing' to explain resistance. He defined threat as the awareness of immanent change in core role structure, noting that clients are often threatened in therapy, when it looks as though they may get more change than they bargained for. Behaviour therapists (for example Meyer et al., 1976) were no strangers to resistance, explaining it in terms of double approach–avoidance conflicts. So the phenomena of self-defeating behaviour and resistance are widely recognised in the world of psychotherapy.

The idea of a dynamic unconscious that works away in the depths of each person, producing more or less costly strategies for the handling of psychological high explosives, was an interesting one. Self-deception and evasion were inevitable costs, and the results might do more harm than good, depending on how much was being contained. Repression per se was not unhealthy. Indeed, Freud saw it as a necessary price that is paid for being human and certainly living in civilised society. As dreaming showed, everybody has an unconscious. But some people have more to contend with than do others. The trauma they have suffered, the quality of parenting and care they have received makes some people have to take drastic (but unconscious) steps to keep the lid on things. The client in therapy is often in conflict about change. You go into therapy saying, in effect, 'I just want to get over my depression, but I want everything else to stay the same'. But life is a complicated package deal. Confronting the reasons why you are depressed will, at the very least, involve examining all sorts of things and some sort of resistance is inevitable. In the view of psychoanalysis, we are all houses divided. The analyst tries to encourage the part of us that wants to change, but has to contend with the part that doesn't. Freud argued that evidence for unconscious repression came from the irrational force with which improving change is resisted in therapy.

Now Freud believed that successful therapy depended on making the unconscious conscious; indeed this was the stated aim of psychoanalysis. It followed that this aim could not be achieved by confronting people with what they were doing. There was no point in rational argument, because the unconscious mind did not obey the laws of logic. (Nevertheless, it is interesting to read the accounts of Albert Ellis (1987), who trained as a psychoanalyst and claimed that rational argument could be used to overcome resistance.) The vehicle for therapeutic change therefore became the relationship between analyst and patient. The analyst focuses principally on the patients' transferences, that is, how they reproduce early patterns of relationships in their contact with the analyst. Patients have to draw on their (unconscious) experience in order to join up the dots presented by the indefinite outline presented by the ambiguous figure of the analyst. The analysts' credo is that this tells of their unconscious phantasies with internalised objects.

Unconscious phantasies

For the object relations theorists, it is our unconscious relations with internalised objects that steer our actions. Beginning in infancy, we develop relationships with the external world, including people. The pattern of these relationships is anticipated and repeated in joint actions (of course, the object relations theorists don't use this concept) with future people and events in our lives. These patterns are set up before we have the use of symbols and language and constitute what are called 'unconscious phantasies'. The use of the term 'phantasy' emphasises two things. Firstly, they are to be distinguished from fantasies, which are conscious daydreams or reveries. Secondly, they are to be distinguished from external reality. It is through them that we see the world; they are constructions or schemas that distort the way things actually are. They are like narratives or scripts (Stoller, 1986) that determine our relationships. In the view of psychodynamic theory, it is also essential that they remain unconscious, because their content would be too disturbing to the person, were they revealed to him.

In therapy, there is always a 'honeymoon period' (Malan, 1979), in which there is a surge of hope and relief at the prospect of dealing with psychological distress. This is followed by resistance, where patients do all they can to prevent the experience of further distress that would follow the unearthing and revealing of unconscious phantasy. We might rage at the way we have been misunderstood and misused, abused by our partner and generally victimised. Perhaps it was the inability to deal with rage and resentment that brought us into therapy in the first place. What we would like is someone to sympathise with us, understand our point of view, ally themselves with us in our fight against an unjust world. We have told ourselves the story of ourselves as victim over and over again. It makes us angry. But perhaps we fail to see the part we have played in our misfortune.

Why do we lay ourselves open to being misused? Why have we not left our partner? Why have we not taken our own 'good advice' on several occasions? The asking of these uncomfortable questions leads to resistance, and it is our strenuous insistence on the truth of our conscious story that has led to the analytic belief in the unconscious. The experience of rage and resentment might be bad enough, but preferable to the sense of desolation and guilt that we might have to face if we recognised the role of our unconscious phantasies in our problems.

For psychoanalysts, understanding people means more than recognising the way things appear to them. It means drawing on what Ricoeur (1970) termed the 'hermeneutics of suspicion' rather than the 'hermeneutics of belief'. The analyst interprets by looking behind and beneath appearances to search for the meaning of conscious experience. The patient's reason cannot be appealed to because it is under the invisible influence of his unconscious. The ego is blackmailed, manipulated and misled. It is told only partial and convenient truths. It cannot be relied upon to know what is really going on, and belief in its testimony must always be balanced by suspicion. The analyst therefore focuses on the way the patient transfers his phantasies onto the analyst and projects into him feelings that are picked up in the counter-transference. The interpretations focus on this joint action. The patient can deny that he positions people so that they feel irritated and invited to reject him. But he cannot deny that the analyst feels this here and now as a result of the transactions in the consulting room. This has to be dealt with as a live issue and cannot be relegated to a theoretical discussion about the past.

A critique of the dynamic unconscious

I think we can see two things here: just how innovative and potentially useful psychoanalytic technique can be and also just how dangerous it can be. The hermeneutics of suspicion are both its strength and its weakness. Its refusal to take at face value the way things appear to people is surely an essential step in any therapeutic enterprise. I cannot be the final authority on what I am doing; my account has to be listened to carefully, but not believed uncritically. The credulous approach (Kelly, 1955) is a vital component of therapeutic listening. The therapist's job is to understand my account, but not to be captured by it – a difficult but necessary balance of taking me seriously, but not at face value. If everybody else thinks I am a self-deceptive, irritating moralist, it will do me no good at all to cling to my story that I am self-sacrificing and nobody understands me. Sooner or later, I am going to have to confront what psychoanalysis construes as the unconscious forces at work in me. But the psychoanalytic way of taking the person seriously is driven by a theory that is very top-heavy in content. In contrast to, say, Kelly's theory, which confines itself to propositions about psychological processes, psychoanalysis has strong propositions concerning the content and nature of the processes. Of course, therapists have to draw on a theoretical framework, either explicit or implicit, in order to make sense of anything people do. We can appreciate how the dynamic unconscious has been invented to explain some of the mysteries of human action. But psychoanalysts know in advance what they are going to find in anybody's unconscious: Freud's oedipal conflicts and Klein's pre-oedipal emotions of envy, hatred, omnipotence and greed. In the tradition of modern science, psychoanalysis sees itself as an enterprise of discovery. It is in the business of finding truths about human nature that transcend culture. But as Merleau-Ponty (1962) insisted, everything in people is both natural *and* cultural. Psychoanalytic theory makes very little allowance for the social constructions of different times. What is regarded as taboo varies enormously and with it, surely, what provides good potential material for repression. So, fifty years ago, gay sexuality was regarded as taboo in a way that it no longer is, and hence would then have been a stronger candidate for repression than it is now.

Both Spinelli (1995) and Westen (1998) point out that there is increasing experimental evidence for the existence of unconscious processes in contemporary psychological literature. However, the evidence for repression and a dynamic unconscious is weak. No one seems to dispute that there are cognitive processes that occur beneath the level of conscious awareness. Skilled behaviour like driving a car or riding a bike call for a 'knowing how' that does not require conscious deliberation once competence is achieved. People cannot say how they do these things. It is difficult to describe to somebody else how you juggle, play a tennis shot or swim so that they can then do it. They have to immerse their body in the activity and practise at it. As Westen (1998) says, there is no reason to doubt that affective processes are similarly preconscious. Feelings of anger, love, jealousy and fear all arise in interactions and confrontations with the world before we think about them. As Wittgenstein (1972) argued convincingly, we cannot describe our emotions. As we saw in Chapter 4, when we tell someone how we feel, we might be doing a number of things (for example looking for sympathy and understanding, bullying or embarrassing) but we are not describing something going on inside us. Westen sees evidence for a dynamic unconscious in studies which showed that discussing unpleasant emotions leads to an immediate increase, but a long-term decrease, in arousal. Keeping oneself unaware of one's feelings is thus a defensive manoeuvre that can be counterproductive. But do we need a concept of repression to account for such findings? Repression assumes that material is first of all conscious and subsequently buried in a 'deeper' region of the mind. The existential alternative instead focuses not on an unconscious mind, but on a pre-reflective body. Here, consciousness, that is, the ability to reflect on things, is a development built on our pre-reflective being-in-the-world. So everything that we do is unconscious to begin with, and only becomes conscious when we reflect and spell out our engagement with the world. What the psychoanalysts think of as unconscious phenomena occur when, for one reason or another, we do not engage in this reflection.

The existential project

Sartre (1958) criticised the concept of an unconscious realm of the mind, governed by its own laws and logic. He contended that the existence of a censor with the attributes proposed by Freud was highly problematic. How does the censor know what would or would not be dangerous should it reach consciousness? There must be some form of consciousness in operation here, in order for the censor to perform its duties effectively. There cannot really be a little executive in each of us, deciding whether or not to throw a switch that allows a thought or wish enough energy to achieve consciousness. Freud was only talking figuratively of course, but this mechanistic metaphor blinds us to the fact that any censoring function must 'know' what it is doing when it relegates material to the unconscious. When we create internal sub-personalities, psychic structures and special states of consciousness, we put beyond the reach of human agency actions for which people are ultimately responsible. The proposition of an unconscious mind leads us to talk of material that is 'buried' and 'deeper' than consciousness. It situates the problem inside a private unreachable realm, in the region of Descartes' ghost. Most importantly, it makes the person unaccountable for his actions. Responsibility is passed to unconscious forces that are beyond reason and control.

Let's consider a hypothetical case. Imagine that somebody you
know continually treats all her friends and acquaintances as if they
are much luckier than she is. In fact, it always looks to you and everybody else that she's rather lazy, and doesn't appreciate the way
everybody else is always doing things for her. She always says how
lucky you are – with your job, your relationships and even your
looks. She doesn't seem to realise that you've had to work at these
things, and it doesn't seem at all like luck to you. But she expects you
and others to treat her like one of life's victims. There is an air of
depression about her, and in her presence you increasingly feel on
your guard and self-conscious. She expects to be able to cry on your
shoulder, even though she never reciprocates with supporting others.
You know one person has told her to get a grip; that, actually, she's
been quite lucky herself. Her response was to cry and sulk, and the
other person ended up feeling cruel and guilty. Now, it's quite possible to formulate this as an issue of unconscious phantasy – she
doesn't know what she's doing, and just can't see that she is driven
by unconscious envy that it is impossible for her to acknowledge.
The way she sees things leads to people treating her badly, and supplies further evidence for her theory that she is badly-used and
unlucky. She is in a vicious circle in which her unconscious phantasy
leads to self-fulfilling prophecies. But what can she do about this?
How is she to change when the problem is rooted in the unreachable
depths of her unconscious? Without psychoanalysis, it seems that she
is doomed to repeat the pattern endlessly.

Self-deception

Another way of looking at this case is to see it as an example not of
repression and unconscious phantasy, but of self-deception. Both
Sartre (1958) and Merleau-Ponty (1962) emphasised that each
person is engaged on an existential project and has developed a
chosen way of being-in-the-world. The preservation of this project
may well entail a degree of self-deception. If I have chosen to see
myself as a victim, one to whom things happen, I will have to deny
my agency in this process and always see the success of others as
mere luck. It is not that material is buried beyond retrieval; rather,
we choose not to look at our intentionality and our way of being-in-
the-world. We all know instances of self-deception in our everyday
lives. We tend to see how other people err, but are blind to the exact
faults in ourselves. Montaigne once said that if you want to know an

individual's shortcomings, notice those that they are sensitive to in others. This projection is just one example of our very skilled (but, sadly, very normal) ability to deceive ourselves. Malan (1979) commented that unconscious phenomena can be construed along a dimension from things that we simply do not acknowledge to things that are deeply buried. For Sartre (1958) everything is at the unacknowledged end of the spectrum. There are aspects of our own psychological processes – our wishes, feelings and thoughts – that, for one reason or other, are unacknowledged.

Fingarette (1969) elaborated this type of approach to self-deception in an analysis that is consistent both with existentialism and the work of the later Wittgenstein. In a critique of Cartesian dualism, he argued that we should not think of consciousness as a mirror reflecting some internal state of mind. When I say that I feel envious of somebody, I am not looking into some inner depths and describing and discovering something I find there. Instead, consciousness is like a skill, an ability to spell things out to ourselves in an inner dialogue. And this skill of course relies on having a vocabulary to hand. Discursive or reflective consciousness thus resembles conversation. Because I am familiar with the concept of envy, and see how it is used in public life, I am able to relate my experience within its framework. But we might simply not have the vocabulary or conversational skills to hand that would enable us to spell things out. In contemporary society, we live in an extended vocabulary dealing with feelings and emotion. It will therefore be easier for us to find words to express ourselves than it would have been for our forebears. Billig (1997) makes a similar argument in his formulation of a 'dialogic unconscious'. He points out how, in everyday talk, people learn the rules of politeness. This involves an awareness of what one should avoid – rudeness. Although this might not be spelt out in reflective consciousness, people have no difficulty in following the rules. Billig (1997) argues that, in this way, rudeness is, in a sense, repressed. Similarly, internal conversations will be conducted in a way that avoids, or 'represses', certain things. It seems to me, though, that this is a rather weak form of repression; it doesn't cover a more active type of self-deception. There is more to self-deception than being unable to spell things out to oneself or bypassing certain contrasting constructions. There is also a more active refusal to spell things out, and this Sartre (1958) saw as an example of what he termed 'bad faith'. Here, it is not that we are not able, but we are unwilling to spell out our engagement with the world.

Sartre championed a view of extreme freedom, in the face of which everybody indulges in a greater or lesser degree of bad faith. Of course, he recognised that we do not possess complete freedom of action – many things prevent us from doing just what we would like to. But we do have the freedom to take a different attitude towards life and in many ways act differently. His contention was that in order to disguise from ourselves the extent of our personal freedom, we devise strategies and excuses that let us off the hook of responsibility. For example, we hide behind identities that we create for ourselves, declare that God or fate have decreed the course of events and believe that we are pushed around by instinctive (and unconscious) forces. 'I don't know what came over me' we might say, as we disavow the sort of lustful or aggressive act that might alternatively be explained in terms of the psychanalytic id. What we relegate as unconscious is a refusal to look at something. It is as though we have gone into a dark room with the searchlight of consciousness and there are some dark corners into which we are afraid to look.

Spinelli (1995) developed the Sartrian account of the unconscious, likening it to dissociation. This denotes splits in consciousness rather than a split between a conscious and an unconscious mind. Consequently, the unconscious is not deeper, more profound or possessed of special causal powers. Rather it is composed of aspects of experience that one disavows. No special mechanism is needed to explain it. All the same, the results of dissociation can be dramatic. We see this in hypnosis, where people can ignore pain and follow post-hypnotic suggestions without remembering them. There is no question here of buried depths coming to the surface, just a dissociation of consciousness that, as it were, allows the right hand to operate without the knowledge of the left. Spinelli (1989, 1995) argues that it is when a person's experience is incongruent with his self-concept that dissociation is called on as a solution. If I think of myself as a kind, considerate person, and find myself acting in a spiteful, vengeful way, what am I to do? Theoretically, I could change or enlarge my core structure to make it permeable to this new behaviour. This, however, is not the route most often taken. So the alternative is to not achieve the gestalt of spiteful and vengeful. If I can't forget the incident, I can perhaps redefine it, bringing other issues into focus and making them figure rather than ground. So I can search for alternative constructions. I can say that I was being honest, I was standing up for myself or the object of my spite deserved to be upset at what I said or did. It is when being spiteful and vengeful is seen as an enduring aspect of my personality, and one that I strenuously deny, that we are likely to talk about unconscious forces acting on me. But this vocabulary unnecessarily mystifies what is happening. The way to understand me is to look at how things appear to me and how I interpret them. Then we can make sense of the lengths I go to in order to deceive myself about what I am feeling and doing.

The pre-reflective body

The notion of repression is particularly appealing when our assumptions about people are governed by Cartesian dualism. If we think of a person's projects as being dictated and planned by an inner entity, a mind, then certain ideas, images and wishes produced by this reflective consciousness have to be examined and shelved because of their disturbing qualities. But the existentialist alternative does not deal in minds and bodies. It proposes that the pre-reflective body is already engaged in the physical and social world before the skill of reflection is acquired. We find ourselves attracted to some people and practices, and repulsed by others. The term 'feeling' properly refers not to some inner emotion, but to sensory contact with the world, and the tone of these feelings indicates the particular nature of our being-in-the-world. It is this pre-reflective contact that has the qualities that Freud saw as the illogical and contradictory properties of the unconscious. But as Merleau-Ponty (1962) argued, everything in the lived world is ambiguous and does not have the clear-cut definition sought in the objective thought that appealed to Freud. Instead of talking of true feelings that are repressed and inside us, Merleau-Ponty keeps his focus on perception, our point of contact with the world:

> The complex is not like a thing that would subsist deep within us and produce its effects on the surface from time to time. Exclusive of the time when it is manifested, it is present only in the way in which the knowledge of a language is present when we are not speaking it. (Merleau-Ponty, 1963: 178)

The lived world is ambiguous, and we are frequently fascinated by what terrifies us, drawn to things that repel us and disgusted by things that also excite us. What we 'really feel' is a mixture of contradictory emotions. Westen (1998) comments that it is surprising that anybody can indulge in pleasurable sexual activity, given that the genitals are organs of excretion – the natural focus of disgust – and the first decade of our lives links genitals with disgusting products. Ambivalence and ambiguity are built into sexuality, and this is particularly evident, Westen (1998) observes, in those patients who are simultaneously strongly repulsed by and attracted to particular activities or body parts. The concept of the 'gestalt' is useful in recognising the ambiguity that is characteristic of the so-called 'unconscious'. Figure and ground can change in a way that accentuates some aspect of the world (for example its excitement) while others (say, its disgusting aspect) are consigned to the background. As Stoller (1986) demonstrates with clinical case studies, what seems thrilling has only to be very slightly modified to become either completely dull or unbearably terrifying. The thought of being tied up during sex might seem very appealing in fantasy, and perhaps more so if the fantasy was acted out with a trusted partner. But any excitement might quickly fade if the partner fails to act the exact part that we have scripted for him. And the excitement would quickly transform into fright if the constraint went beyond consent and one *really* had no control over the proceedings. Any thrill, like going to a horror movie, is only pleasantly exciting when we know that we are not actually in the situation. This applies whether it is a haunted house, a murder mystery or in the sea with a shark. The thrill feeds on the ambiguity of a danger at a safe distance, and sexual thrill is no different. Stoller (whose work moved from a psychoanalytic to a more ethnographic and phenomenological approach) claimed that sexual thrill is often based on potentially terrifying scenarios.

It is in our perception, our transactions with the world, that ambiguity resides. Very slight variations change the gestalt entirely, as elements in our perceptual field move from figure to background and vice versa:

> This unconscious is to be sought not at the bottom of ourselves, not behind the back of our 'consciousness', but in front of us, as articulations of our field. (Merleau-Ponty, 1968: 180)

So for Merleau-Ponty, there is no unconscious mind with causal power. Instead, the pre-reflective body articulates its perception, foregrounding some aspects of the field and making others background. In a sense, what is background remains unconscious. Here we see both Merleau-Ponty's interest in psychoanalysis, and also his rejection of the deep, fundamental and causal properties of the unconscious. For Merleau-Ponty (1962), Freud was quite correct in seeing a latent sexual meaning in dreams, but wrong in attributing such pre-eminence to it. Sexuality is like an 'atmosphere' that always potentially pervades the body-subjects' dealings in the world. But if unconscious forces do not cause us to see things in certain ways, how are we to account for individuals' articulation of the perceptual field in certain characteristic ways? Spinelli's proposition that the preferred gestalt is influenced by a person's self-concept (I prefer the Kellian notion of self-theory) finds support in many everyday experiences. The conflict between how one experiences oneself and what one believes oneself to be is frequently resolved by a refusal to recognise an experience as one's own. We see this conflict clearly in the diaries of British actor and comedian Kenneth Williams (Butt and Langdridge, 2003). Williams kept a diary for over forty years of his life. They were found after his death (probably from suicide) in 1988. The editor of the diaries (Davies, 1994) observed that, in many respects, the diaries resembled the dialogue one might have at the end of the day with one's partner or a close confidante. Williams lived alone and instead confided his impressions of other people and life generally to his diaries. So we hear a range of different voices and opinions expressed in the fairly spontaneous mode that we associate with conversation. Like anybody in a number of different joint actions, Williams could be funny, depressed, spiteful, angry and sanctimonious in turn. Nonetheless, we see the fashioning of a self-theory; that of a conservative (and indeed Conservative) man, strongly moralistic and unforgiving in his assessment of both others and himself. This, then, is the result of reflective consciousness, a theory that evolves and is refined over time as a product of his interpretation of who he is. But how does this *me* measure up to the *I*, the pre-reflective actor that it is trying to define?

Williams was an intelligent and articulate man who covered many aspects of his life in his diaries and pondered honestly on many of the great issues of life. But one area that is dealt with very sparsely is his gay sexuality. We know from many of the TV documentaries on his life that have been broadcast in recent years that he was a gay man who at one time had a long-term sexual relationship. He also had a variety of sexual adventures in Morocco, which he visited in the company of Joe Orton, an openly gay playwright. In the 1950s, he was a central comic character on a radio show who used a gay code that was clearly decipherable to a gay audience. Now it is easy to appreciate the secrecy of a gay man in the Britain of the 1950s and early 1960s. Same-sex relationships between men were illegal, and men did go to prison for indulging in gay sex. But a casual reader of the diaries might conclude that Williams was simply homophobic. He often referred to gay men with scorn and intolerance. This internalised homophobia cannot be explained in terms of prevailing discourses that permeate the person, writing on the docile body with disciplinary power. Of course he was swimming in a very hostile social current, but he was also situated in the relatively tolerant acting community in which many other gay friends existed more easily. His dislike of his own sexuality (some might say, his self-loathing) represented an inability to accommodate his sexuality into his moralistic self-theory. In the diaries, he makes veiled references to masochistic masturbation fantasies and declares that he must control himself; he must live the life of a celibate. He despised those who submitted to their appetites and this appears to be a central feature in his condemnation of openly gay men.

Williams thus disavowed his pre-reflective sexual attraction to other men. The attraction was something over which he had no control; he found himself in the world in this way. We can try to say why we are attracted to this man or that woman, but this pre-reflective engagement is something we may well find difficult to capture in words. People resort to metaphor, poetry, music and dance to try to express their love, finding prose inadequate for the task. The pre-reflective attraction between body-subjects is something that predates language and symbol usage. But as I have argued before, everything in people is both natural and cultural. Reflective consciousness plays back on the pre-reflective body. Feelings of loathing and disgust led in Williams' case to what seemed to him like the only solution to his problem – rigid self-control and sexual abstinence. He thus disavowed his sexuality – it had an alien quality to it that he could not make his own.

Personal responsibility and the unconscious

The focus of convenience of the dynamic unconscious was conversion hysteria; the manifesting of psychological distress in physical complaints. The range of the concept stretches to include a variety of phenomena that are apparent in everyday life but seen par excellence in neurotic processes. The effect of proposing the existence of unconscious motivation is that the person is seen as no longer responsible for his action. The cause of it is buried deep in a dark region of the mind and beyond his control. This sort of explanation is accepted because of the Cartesian assumptions that are behind both orthodox and folk psychology. When we separate mind from body, we then have to ask how the former kick-starts the latter into action when necessary. How is it that when we experience a wish, a thought or a feeling, this mind state becomes translated into behaviour? Psychological textbooks define motivation as factors that 'energise and direct behaviour'. They then devote sections to motivation and emotion that often overlap with issues of personality. As we have noted, the science of personality is centrally concerned with motivation: why people act as they do. But the textbook chapters on motivation are frequently partly based in biology. When our starting point is not a disembodied mind, but a body-subject, the problems of motivation are reframed. They are replaced by different questions that focus on the way things appear to people, and their reasons for action in the light of these appearances. So explanations in terms of forces are replaced by a quest for understanding in phenomenological terms. The energising of our behaviour does not require explanation when we see the person as naturally in motion, always engaged on some project or other. But the direction of our action is another matter – why we choose to do some things rather than others. Now, because our existential projects are in the main pre-reflective, it is not always immediately apparent to us why we act as we do. Because reflection is a skill that depends on the vocabularies we have to hand to spell out to ourselves what we are doing, we might be unable to articulate the reasons for our action. It might also be the case that we would prefer not to recognise what we are doing. As we have seen, it was in order to address these issues that the concept of the dynamic unconscious was invented.

When we call on the concept of 'unconscious motivation', we try to avoid attributing blame to people. But as Keen (1975) points out, the use of psychiatric diagnoses does not in the end succeed in avoiding blame. Clarity of meaning is obscured and resentment and blame still attach themselves to those said to be suffering from mental illnesses. We see this in the everyday use of psychiatric terms as insults. Neurotic, psychotic, hysterical, psychopathic – all are used as insults in everyday speech. On the other hand, if we talk about choice, we see people as responsible for what they are doing. 'You've made your bed, so you can lie on it' we think. But this is a very harsh and unforgiving attitude. It assumes that people make choices deliberately and have a clear vision of where their choices will lead them. In fact neither is the case. What is needed, surely, is an appreciation of the complex nature of choice and responsibility without attributing blame. Kelly (1969a) provided a very nice summary of the nature of the existential project (see also Holland, 1970, 1977; Butt, 1997):

- People do not choose between logical alternatives, or the alternatives that we the observers see, but between the options as they see them.
- We do not choose on the basis of simply gaining pleasure or avoiding pain. Instead we make the choices that help us anticipate – those that make most sense to us.
- We do not choose freely in the sense that our options are often restricted by circumstances. This means we often have to choose the best course we see between several unpleasant alternatives.
- We never know exactly where our choices will lead us.

Taken together, these dimensions of choice offer a way of understanding what people do which recognises both their responsibility for action and the way this is limited by their social and psychological circumstances. Their behaviour is not caused by what happens to them, but it is an expression of their way of being-in-the-world. If we return to the example of Kenneth Williams, today, we can see many options other than the 'giving into lust versus total abstinence' that appeared to be the options he saw open to him. I stress 'today' because we inhabit a social climate that is more tolerant of the plurality of sexual expression, and we should not see Williams' choice as due simply to a lack of individual imagination. The choices he made led in many respects to his leading an unhappy life. But he could not see into the future. Neither could he make decisions that did not fit into his self-theory. He had to make the choices that made sense to him. The issue of personal change is central to the psychology of personality, and it is to this issue that I will turn in the final chapter.

9

Psychological Reconstruction

At the beginning of this book, I made the point that one of the concerned parents of personality theory is clinical psychology. The aim of understanding people has a pragmatic focus in personal change and psychotherapy. With the exception of trait theory, all personality theories have implications for how to bring about personal change in therapy. People in distress present the clearest case of the need for a theory that makes sense of their suffering and offers a route to psychological reconstruction. As we saw in Chapter 8, it is difficult to see psychological distress as like physical illness. Personal change is not like overcoming an infection or recovering from physical trauma. It usually involves changing the way we see things and our comfortable ways of acting. It often means that we have to question our implicit theories about both other people and ourselves. It is therefore not surprising that clients practise various techniques of evasion in therapy. As van Deurzen (2002) argues, 'evasion' is perhaps a better term than 'resistance'. It denotes a milder form of non-cooperation but nevertheless captures the way in which people move away from confronting well-ingrained and sedimented aspects of their conduct. Different psychological therapies base their models of psychological disturbance and change on different personality theories, each with their formulation of human agency. These different models indicate the use of different methods in therapy. In particular, they make different use of the therapeutic relationship. In some, for example psychoanalysis and Rogerian therapy, the therapeutic relationship is seen as the main instrument of change, even though this is conceptualised quite differently in each of them. In others, like cognitive-behavioural therapy, it is almost incidental, the main focus being a joint effort at directing change outside the consulting room.

However, despite these widely differing theories and practices, research indicates that all approaches are more or less equally effective (Smith and Glass, 1977). Of course, what counts as 'effective' is contentious. The very notion of effectiveness has been imported from medicine, and some have argued that it is inappropriate when considering psychological change (Bannister, 1980). Nonetheless, it remains clear that there will be some people who will benefit from each of the psychological therapies on offer. I have never met a therapist who claimed that her approach is the only one that works. All acknowledge that there are people who can make better use of some than others, and that some types of problem appear to be best dealt with by one therapy rather than another. From the perspective of existential phenomenology, this is not at all surprising. Only when we think of treatment or therapy as something that is applied in a mechanistic way to passive patients would we expect any simple results concerning 'effectiveness' to follow. Personal change surely depends on what sense the client can make of the procedures of therapy. As Kelly (1955) insisted, it is the client who interprets, not the therapist. The therapist may make so-called 'interpretations' but it is how these statements are understood by the client, how they are assimilated into her meaning system, that will influence things. Everything is filtered through the way things appear to her or, in Kelly's terminology, her construct system.

So in this final chapter, I don't want to debate the strengths and weaknesses of different therapy systems. I don't think we are ever going to end up with one form of therapy that suits everybody. It would be naive to think that therapists of a particular school would pack up their operations because some research appeared to indicate that what they were doing was a waste of time. The outcomes of research can and will always be interpreted differently, especially when consumers of it have strong interests in reading it in a particular way. So it is fruitless to pursue the effectiveness debate in a way that mirrors that of the effectiveness of a particular drug or medical procedure. Instead, I want to think about the whole therapy project and consider it in the light of the existential phenomenological perspective on the person. I will start by looking at the increasing popularity of therapy and counselling in today's society. I will argue that we cannot understand this development by looking inside people and focusing on individuals alone. We have to set this phenomenon in its social context to appreciate it.

The rise of therapy

At the beginning of the twentieth century, no one had heard of psychotherapy. One hundred years later, it has become a central feature in the late modern world. Spinelli (1994) tells us that 30,000 people in the UK earned a living from therapy, 270,000 more practised in the voluntary sector and 2.5 million clients used counsellors at work. It would appear that in the intervening century, we had discovered a well of psychological distress that had gone unrecognised hitherto. As we have seen, in World War I, soldiers were executed for suffering from what is now known as PTSD. Children were routinely physically abused and, it seems, often sexually abused as well. Private suffering was not recognised in the same way as it is today. Life was harder in most respects and stoicism was admired as a strategy for coping with harsh circumstances and life's unfairness. One hundred years later, things are very different. Not only is there a proliferation of therapists and counsellors, but their vocabulary has found its way into everyday talk and has become commonplace. Most people have now heard of anorexia, bulimia and obsessional compulsive disorder. People talk about being stressed out, abused and of getting in touch with their feelings. The shelves of bookshops are filled with works on self-help and recovery. At first glance, it seems as though this is an unqualified advance in both scientific thinking and humanitarian interest. We now recognise people's psychological problems in a way that relieves them of blame and responsibility. Consequently, more people come forward with problems that need therapy. We now know that there has been an enormous clinical iceberg; what we had seen as the incidence of psychological distress hid a mass of undeclared problems that we've now discovered. We can see an enormous increase in the demand for therapy, and what is needed is the training of more psychotherapists and counsellors.

However, as we saw when we considered the writings of Foucault, it is possible to take a more cynical view of these developments. We could see the twentieth century as the culmination of the intrusion of disciplinary power. The rise in therapy could be seen as evidence of the triumph of implanted surveillance. Psychological distress is a construction rather than a discovery. The therapy industry could be seen as selling its wares to a gullible public. The fact that people want therapy does not, after all, demonstrate that it is good for them. People prefer prepared foods to natural vegetables; they are tastier and we want more and more of them. But this certainly does not mean that they are more nutritious. The job of an industry is to sell its products; to find a niche in the market. Psychotherapy, it could be argued, is no different. Its practitioners wholeheartedly believe in its value and recommend it in good faith. But they are as likely as anybody else to be the victims of self-deception All the most convincing salespeople are sincere and believe in the value of their products. They are too close to what they do to evaluate it clearly. Through psychotherapy we see the creeping influence of a medical framework and through it surveillance into all our lives. We used to call people 'inadequate', 'immoral' and 'evil'. Now we say they are suffering from various psychological conditions (see Szasz, 1970). The framework of explanation is all that has changed; a new social construction has been applied that gives a veneer of tolerance but hides a relentless and intrusive strategy of control.

From the perspective of this critique, the individual's freedom of action and ultimately thought is in fact threatened by the therapy ethic. Freud thought it possible to distinguish between common un-happiness and neurotic misery. But now everything is neurotic misery. We have lost sight of the problems inherent in existence, and think that there is a remedy for every problem through talking about our troubles. We hear about a tragedy in the news, and the next thing we hear is that everybody even tangentially concerned will have access to counsellors. Presumably, we are meant to be reassured: 'so that's OK then, everything will be fine once the counsellors have been parachuted in'. We want to believe that once victims have let off steam, everything will carry on as before. Of course, those involved in counselling and therapy realise that it's not quite like this, but the news coverage reproduces the myth of the administration of the balm of counselling that will heal the psychologically shaken. Professionals are in charge of the actual counselling, but they do not and cannot control its image in the press and how it is received and interpreted by the general public. In the public eye, psychological expertise and therapeutic potency have become magnified. Smail (1993) argues that one of the effects of (and perhaps one reason for) this is that it takes our attention away from the dreadful lives people often lead. It moves the focus to inside people when it should properly be on living conditions. We concentrate on mending the individuals rather than addressing their situation.

So we can see that there is a spectrum of possible ways of thinking about the proliferation of therapy. At one end, there is the story of the advance of orthodox modern science: psychology gradually discovers more about the human psyche. At the other, a social constructionist critique: a vocabulary of distress is constructed that directs our attention misleadingly onto or into individuals. There is, I think, a truth in each position. The fact that there appears to be more psychological distress around cannot be thought of as a simple discovery. This must say something about our social world and the particular shape it gives to our experience. Society precedes the construction of the individual. In fashioning ourselves, we have to draw on the social practices in which we are immersed, one of which is language. But to say that selves are socially constructed does not mean that they are not real enough once constructed. We cannot discount people's experience, and the fact is that people now evidently see themselves differently from how they did in the recent past. An understanding of this entails an appreciation of both social and individual construction in the production of meaning. Social constructionism does have something important to say about individuals' experience, but as Craib argues (1998), this does not mean it has *everything* to say. The increased interest in psychotherapy and counselling must reflect an increased focus on feelings in everyday life. People appear to be more aware of feelings, or at least more prepared to talk about them now, and one of the notable features of contemporary life is a change in the expression of emotions and feelings. Let us now consider the experience of feeling and emotion, and look at how both social and individual construction play a part in it.

Emotions and feelings

There is certainly a change in how people express their emotions in today's society. I will draw my examples of this from the UK, because it is the society I know best. Perhaps because of the stereotyped English as stoical and cut off from their feelings, this is a context in which the phenomenon is most pronounced and noticeable. In 1997, Diana, Princess of Wales died in a car crash. The public outpouring of grief was remarkable. Mountains of flowers adorned newly erected shrines and inconsolable members of the general public sobbed by the roadside as the funeral procession made its way across London. People who had never had any contact at all with her made it very clear that they felt desolate and abandoned. It was extraordinary enough that people should feel so close to someone they did not know. But that this should be expressed in the way that it was was astonishing. The royal family found itself out of step with the public mood as its members remained in seclusion. The Queen even had to make a TV broadcast to assure people that she was grieving just as they were. No state funeral had ever been like this before. The unwritten rules concerning the expression of emotion appeared to have been changed overnight. Since around this time we have witnessed the erection of roadside floral tributes in memory of road accident victims. Following a tragic event, we see TV pictures of people crying and hugging each other. Not relatives or friends, but people who just live in the vicinity or have travelled there to express their grief and sympathy. We are assured that 'trained counsellors' are on hand to help them. If the tragedy is a murdered child, we see would-be lynch mobs, almost foaming at the mouth as they attack police vans carrying the accused to and from court. Strangely, the dignity of the families directly involved contrasts strongly to the incontinent rage of the mob. New terms have been coined, 'road rage' and 'air rage', to describe presumably common contemporary phenomena.

How are we to make sense of all this? The folk psychology that is reproduced in the tabloid newspapers is likely to talk of people feeling things more deeply, or perhaps being in touch with their feelings. The culture of emotional repression has been replaced by one of emotional expression. Such explanations rely on a hydraulic and dualistic image of the person. If we think emotions are suppressed and denied discharge, resulting in mounting pressure, then it sounds healthier when a safety valve is released. When feelings are buried in an unconscious mind, they are not recognised. Yet they bubble away, seeking discharge or displacement. Now it is important not to confuse this populist account with anything in psychoanalysis. Freud recognised a need for repression and contemporary analysts would not endorse simple hydraulic models of the person. What we are talking about here is the way social representations of psychological theory become assimilated into 'common sense'. Theories are raided very selectively for those components that seem to explain or authenticate the phenomena under scrutiny. The lesson that seems to have been taken from a century of therapy, rightly or wrongly, is that emotions are better out than in. Once again, we see that psychologists are not in control of how their theories are drawn on. But emotions do not lie there 'inside' us awaiting outward expression. Certainly we can measure physiological correlates of anger, fear and excitement, but we must not confuse these physiological states with the emotions themselves. The same physiological base can be associated with a variety of identified emotions (Schacter and Singer, 1962). The different way in which people express emotions cannot be explained in terms of the simple release of repression. Physiological states are diffuse and ambiguous, whereas emotional displays are clear and constitute the grounds on which emotions are defined.

In considering the philosophy of the later Wittgenstein (Chapter 4), we saw that we are not in a position to be able to describe inner feelings. Emotional expression is essentially a public rather than a private event. Our consciousness is turned outwards onto the world, and we communicate with others in conversations of both words and gestures. We read each other by both listening to what is said and looking at what is done. We also pay close attention to the way in which things are said and done. We note how other people connect with the world by appreciating their actions and their context. Because we share a common world, we can assess what things mean to them. Emotional expression is one of the key ways in which we communicate with each other. Through the process of interpreting others' constructions, we reach an assessment of their 'state of mind', as well as whether this is intelligible and rational. Understanding others involves not just hearing their words, but appreciating the tone of their connection with the world. It is here that emotions play a vital role. In any society, there have to be implicit rules about what is appropriate emotional expression and what various displays mean. Harré and Gillett (1994) emphasised the social nature of emotions and how rules of display vary from one society to another. Writing a few years before the Diana funeral, they contrasted the rules of emotional display at British and East Mediterranean funerals. They point out that the extravagant display of emotion at the latter cannot be taken to mean that grief is felt more keenly in Greece or Israel than in the UK. Similarly, we cannot conclude that people in Britain today feel more deeply than they did a decade ago. What has changed are the rules of expression, what is taken as a meaningful demonstration of a way of being-in-the-world. Harré and Gillett cite the research of Stearns and Stearns (1988) that traced the history of the usage of emotional words by English speakers over the modern period. They found that at the beginning of this period, 300 years ago, the use of words like anger was defined principally in terms of a person's conduct. By the middle of the nineteenth century, though, the focus had shifted onto individuals' feelings. This was accompanied by a feminisation of emotion, which was increasingly seen as the province of women. The 'rational men versus emotional women' myth presumably has its origins in this period. Men were expected to be stoical and in control of their feelings. Women, on the other hand, were allowed emotional extravagance. Bringing feelings under control was both a strength and a virtue. The change in emotional expression that we have seen in recent times shows something of a revision of this prizing of stoicism. The gender-specificity of emotions that Harré and Gillett noted ten years ago now seems less clear. Both men and women grieve openly, can be angry and generally 'in touch with their feelings'.

Social and personal construction

This is the social context in which we have to understand the increasing use of therapy and counselling. The fact that more people are seeking therapy does not mean that there is more abuse, trauma or general unhappiness now than there was in the past. It indicates the framework within which people now make sense of their lives. Changing modes of emotional expression, coupled with the late modern emphasis on the self (see Chapter 7) and the rise of expert systems like therapy, encourage people to reflect on themselves and their feelings in new ways. Just as there are now new regimes of the body that are evident in the proliferation of exercise plans and gyms, so there are new psychological regimes that are manifested in the rise of therapy. We reflect on, worry about and make new demands of ourselves in ways that would have seemed strange to our forebears. We are less prepared to live with pain and are less likely to 'grin and bear it'. We have greater expectations and claim more from life. Disembedded from the ties of traditional society, we invest in a series of pure relationships. This centring of relationships on personal fulfilment is more exciting but inevitably raises questions for us about exactly what we want and who we are. This new pattern of living therefore brings with it both new opportunities and new insecurities. Therapy and counselling seem to offer the ways of either changing or living with ourselves that are particularly important in the late modern world.

How we feel and what we think cannot be separated from the social currents in which we swim. The meanings we bestow on things are not individual products, but are co-constituted with others both on a macro- and a micro-level. The micro-level refers to our immediate social contacts – our joint action with others who we meet on a day-to-day basis. The macro-level refers to distal rather than proxi-mal factors – the social structures and practices that everywhere surround us. It is useful here to remember Berger and Luckmann's dialectical model of the person and society. We interpret our experi-ence in the frameworks provided by objectivations like road rage, stress and abuse. These concepts are ready to hand and make sense of experience through drawing on the discourse of individual rights. It is only within such interpretive frameworks that we can feel badly used or angry at others' infringements of our rights. Such objec-tivations, along with the discourses in which they are framed, are internalised and then influence our own actions in the moment of externalisation. Other people validate our constructions because they too are immersed in the same social world with its taken-for-granted assumptions. But Berger and Luckmann's (1967) model differs from psychological varieties of social constructionism in that it allows for a personal as well as a social phase in the construction of meaning. In externalisation, new narratives and identities are fash-ioned as people's experience resonates with that of others. This is not a simple 'top-down' model in which we are passive subjects implanted with ideologies and discourses.

Narratives and social construction

Plummer's (1995) work on the development of new sexual stories in late modernity is a good example of Berger and Luckmann's dialectic in operation. Through the concept of narrative, Plummer manages to capture both personal and social phases in the construction of mean-ing. It highlights the co-constitution of meaning as well as the way in which self and identity are constructed in reflective consciousness. Although he concentrates on sexual stories, he makes clear that this focus is but one example of how identities are shaped by narrative structures. He notes a proliferation of narratives with a sexual theme in the late twentieth century. I will focus here on two of these that con-cern coming out and sexual abuse. Gay sexuality and sexual abuse are not new; people have always been attracted to others of the same sex and Freud's patients were telling him tales of sexual abuse over a hun-dred years ago. What is new is the way in which these phenomena are reported and received in public life. There has been a definite resis-tance to hearing these accounts in even the recent past, and we can see that these stories definitely have their time. The criminalisation of same-sex relations between men and the disbelief of the extent of sexual abuse meant that these stories could not be told or received in the way that they are now. The narrative spans both personal and social worlds. Although all these stories can be seen as originating in the externalisation of private experience and indeed pain, they have achieved an objectivation denied in the past, and are internalised and reproduced as they chime with the experience of other individuals. This process requires 'coaxers', appropriate media and an interactive social world to receive the stories. The accounts would not be in the public realm if it were not for therapists, counsellors and interviewers who coax and encourage individuals to dwell on and publicise their experience. The increased range of available media makes the wide distribution of these accounts possible. An increased number of TV channels, magazines catering for every interest and of course the internet allow these stories to be consumed by a large and varied audience. A story reaches a sort of take-off velocity when it is received by people who are not only sympathetic, but see and reframe their own experience in new terms. They 'realise' that they too have been abused or their sexuality is not as simple as they had previously assumed. Self-help and recovery groups are formed and new identities fashioned as the stories are reproduced and elaborated.

Plummer (1995) identifies a process of transformation that people often go through when they relate tales of suffering. To begin with, there is the experience of private suffering, or the recognition of pain not fully acknowledged. The bearing of a dreadful secret and the weight of lonely suffering are then relieved as the problem is translated into the language of recovery, therapy or political action. This is frequently experienced as an epiphany, or crucial turning point, at which the sufferer feels that she has been transformed by the telling of her story. A negative self-image is transformed into a positive identity as the person is supported by others in therapy, a recovery group or political movement. Obviously, there are differences between, on the one hand, stories of rape and abuse and, on the other, those of coming out. But there are parallels too. Whereas the gay individual who comes out finds her support in the gay community, the victim of abuse is helped by a therapeutic intervention. But the successful outcome always involves the adoption of a new positive identity. As van Deurzen-Smith (1995: 202) observes, therapy with abuse victims involves more than recognition of the wrong done to them: 'The art of good psychotherapy is to find a balance between recognising hurt and discovering the strength to cope with it.' Successful therapy does not leave the person with the identity of victim, feeling wronged and seeking vengeance. It helps the person to reconstrue their past and move on.

In the telling of a story, one both finds and makes oneself. The finding is the acknowledgement of one's pre-reflective connection with the world. This is what is meant by being 'in touch with one's feelings'. The making is the interpretation of this in reflecting upon it and adopting one construction rather than another. The lived world, in the form of our pre-reflective actions, cannot be ignored, but it is open to alternative constructions. When we elaborate a narrative of our lives, we develop a story line that fixes the interpretation and, in so doing, make an identity for ourselves. The core of our being is not an inner entity that predates our being-in-the-world, but just such a narrative construction (Butt et al., 1997b). But calling it a construction does not imply that it is ephemeral or fragile. A self-narrative is a theory that influences our future perception and construction. We rely on it as a base on which to build and from which to make sense of the world. It is therefore resistant to radical change and, as we have seen, produces resistance or evasion in psychotherapy. What is interesting about Plummer's narratives is their transformative potential. Convincing stories have the power to change people's lives. They do not float above the social world, providing a narrative smoothing that merely supplies a way of looking at things. Instead:

> Story production and consumption is an empirical social process involving a stream of joint actions in local contexts themselves bound into wider negotiated social worlds. Texts are connected to lives, actions, contexts and society. (Plummer, 1995: 24)

Adopting new narratives offers a way of changing our lives.

Recently, the British TV Channel 4 broadcast a programme entitled *The Real Linda Lovelace*. Linda Lovelace was the star of porn movies in the late 1960s. She was also an articulate advocate of a libertarian anti-censorship campaign. However, ten years or so later, she proclaimed that she had been the victim of abuse and in fear of her life while in the porn industry. She became a born-again Christian and a leading figure in the feminist campaign for censorship. Because this was such an extreme reversal of her position, there was naturally scepticism on the part of the publishers approached with her biography. It was insisted that she take a lie detector test to settle the issue. This indicated that she was not apparently lying about suffering abuse and living in fear, and her account was subsequently published.

Now this reliance on lie detection is based on the premise that we can in some way get back to what really happened. Either she was or was not telling the truth about it, and there are no other possible alternatives. But memories can never be simply more or less accurate representations of the past. They are filtered through our current system of meanings or constructs. I might relate my earliest memory in good faith and pass any lie detection test. But this does not mean that I have successfully and accurately reconstructed the past. Memories do not simply reside in our brains waiting to be recalled. We rehearse them, tell ourselves stories based on them and elaborate them. As time passes, the way in which we see things changes as we develop new narratives. We are in no position to say what 'really' happened, even though we truthfully record our recollections to the best of our ability. Lovelace's sincerity tells us not about the past, but about her construction of it, and it was this construction that had radically changed.

What might have happened in the intervening years that accounts for this radical repositioning? No doubt many things at a personal level, but certainly there had been important changes in social life. The 1960s had been an iconoclastic decade. Increased wealth, the acceleration in the development of youth culture and spending power, 'flower power' and the anti-war movement all contributed to an increased confidence and rebelliousness in young people in the affluent and developed countries of the west. This was the climate in which Lovelace worked in the porn industry in New York. The 1970s saw the beginning of the women's movement and the raising of feminist consciousness. This was the ground in which the rape and abuse stories flourished. The porn industry was one of the main targets of the early women's movement. It was seen as encouraging rape and abuse. It was against this new narrative that Lovelace made and found her self-identity. It appeared to her as a discovery, a personal revelation, but we can see that it was also conditioned by the new narratives in the social world. This is the sort of epiphany that Plummer noted; a person reconstrues her experience in the light of the new narrative and a sense of injustice is alleviated as she finds support in a new identity. However, the development of this new narrative is not on its own a satisfactory explanation of Lovelace's epiphany – there is no causal relationship here. Rather, it is a necessary, though not a sufficient, condition for it. I doubt that she could have had her revelation in a social vacuum. If it were not for the discourses of feminism, it is hard to see how she could have come to her new conclusions. The lived world is always ambiguous and will afford many interpretations. As Ihde (1986) says, these are occasioned by stories we hear and tell ourselves. We find meanings most readily through the narratives that surround us.

However, the stories that we might key into only provide the tools for personal change. They give us frameworks on which to draw in the fashioning of personal narratives. But we cannot predict who will and will not make use of them. Not everybody looks back and decides that they have been abused, even though they might have been exposed to similar or even worse circumstances. We can understand people better when we appreciate the social world in which they are embedded, but this will not lead to a sequential causal explanation. We have only to think of Kenneth Williams to underline this point. Williams was unfortunate enough to be a gay man brought up in the dreadfully homophobic atmosphere of the mid-twentieth century. His dislike and intolerance of his own sexuality was a common phenomenon with gay men of his generation. But some in his social circle managed to defy convention. Joe Orton, Williams' friend, was not ashamed of his sexuality in the way that Williams was. And when the coming out narrative took off in the 1970s, Williams did not draw support from it and come out himself. He could not make this story his own.

Understanding and being-in-the-world

Understanding people, then, includes appreciating aspects of the social world but it means more than this. It involves seeing how things appear to them and how they interpret them. Social constructionism has added to our understanding, but leaves the project unfinished. As sociologists, Berger and Luckmann (1967) and Plummer (1995) focus on the social aspect of change. They do not explicitly theorise the personal aspect. Nonetheless, their interpretive sociology leaves room for a psychology of the individual. The existential approach gives us a psychology that nicely complements their work, emphasising individuals' existential projects.

The concept of being-in-the-world spans the personal and social worlds of people, transcending the person–world dualism. It recognises that while people are all different, they are also more alike than different. It is because we are all human body-subjects that we have such a degree of commonality. Keen (1975: 108) sums this up very neatly:

We often assume that our minds are private compartments, known to others only to the extent that we choose to share their contents with others. We recognise that we share a common world with others, but we seem also to assume that this commonality is the *result* of our sharing our private mental contents with one another. Quite the opposite assumption is possible: the commonality of the world is not the result of our sharing our experience, but the *basis* of our doing so. My world is like yours, not because we have shared privacy, it was already like yours, and it is only because of this prior similarity that a sharing of private perspectives on it is possible.

Human embodiment gives us a grasp on time and space that is unique in the animal kingdom. It is the basis for the co-construction of meaning that is essential to everyday interactions. Imagine trying to programme a computer to carry out any of the mundane everyday negotiations with others that we take for granted. Walking along a busy street we naturally conduct ourselves so as to avoid bumping into others, moving without thinking into free spaces. The congested road system in the UK only functions at all because of the way in which people pre-reflectively read and interpret others' intentions and anticipate accordingly. What is extraordinary is that there are not many more accidents. The rules are extremely difficult to define, and depend on the execution of so many social acts in which each person responds to ever-changing conditions in a flow of joint action. All this negotiation can only take place because we are beings in the same world. This is the social aspect of being-in-the-world. But we are also beings in different worlds, in that we each perceive and construe in more or less idiosyncratic ways. We all inhabit the same geographical space, but not the same phenomenological space. What might be figure to me might well be ground to you. The events we encounter will have acquired different meanings for each of us, and we each pick out those features in the field that have significance for us. Similarly, we are all time-beings, yet live in time in different ways. Each of us has developed her own individual existential project; a chosen way of being-in-the-world. As we have seen, memory is not a more or less faithful recording of the past. We construct our past as much as it constructs us. People can look back resentfully, wistfully, guiltily or contentedly. Merleau-Ponty (1962) found Sartre's (1958) insistence that 'we are condemned to freedom' too extreme. But he did contend that we are inevitably 'condemned to meaning' (1962: xix). The meanings or constructions that we bestow on the world speak of our particular projects. Our anticipations of the future can be characteristically fearful, hopeful or filled with excitement. The way in which the same world appears can be quite different.

The way people see things, the way they feel and the way they act are all expressions of the way they are in the world. It is characteristic of each of us and what we have come to think of as the self. Understanding people therefore means understanding the way they are in the world. It is clear that personal change will always be most difficult when it implies fundamental change in one's being-in-the-world. What is central to a particular individual will not necessarily be evident to observers. What looks like a simple lack of social skill to the therapist might represent a way of being that rules out piecemeal change. Carl was someone who was shy and wanted something done about it. But he divided people into two kinds: aggressive, insensitive and irritating people, whom he despised, and sensitive, considerate people like himself. His whole way of being revolved around this sense of self that governed his interactions. In many ways, he looked down on others with their social clumsiness. In this sense, his own behaviour was very skilled, even though it brought him little happiness. Therapeutic intervention here has to be based on an understanding of the client. There would be no point in trying to teach Carl to listen more carefully, mesh his conversations with others more appropriately and make more eye contact. This would be to miss the point. The aim of therapy is a psychological reconstruction. For some people for whom their shyness is a relatively simple insensitivity and social clumsiness, social skills training might be just the set of techniques that enable them to transform their lives. Drawing their attention to how they might express themselves better and getting them to think about how other people construe them would be an appropriate course of action. But not for Carl. He needed to reflect on what he was doing; on his project in the world. He had settled into a way of being that didn't work well for him, but was predicated on his theory of himself and others, his being-in-the-world. As Kelly (1969a) argued, people are not simply pleasure-seeking. In this sense, they are not rational or logical, and it can appear that they are self-destructive and in the grip of unconscious forces. Certainly Carl had not deliberated on his life project, but this does not mean that it is in principle beyond his reach. We might expect evasion, but this is because radical change has far-reaching implications, and this is never going to be easy to carry out. Nevertheless, successful intervention must centre on getting him to think about the cost of what he is doing. We can call this 'making the unconscious conscious', or 'getting someone to work with their construct system rather than being worked by it', depending on our theoretical perspective. But whatever we call it, encouraging people to think about what they are doing and accept some responsibility for it is not going to be easy.

The point of understanding

Understanding, then, is an essential prerequisite for bringing about psychological change. How we conceptualise the therapeutic relationship is very important here. Psychodynamic therapies work towards a parent–infant model, because of their focus in the transference. Cognitive-behavioural therapists see themselves as having the expertise of teachers who draw on the principles of cognitive social learning theory. Existential therapists have a different kind of educational model for their therapy. Van Deurzen (2002) sees the therapy session as like an individual tutorial. Spinelli (1994) talks about both being with and being for the client. In both these models, the therapist has an expertise that centres on her focus on the life-world, and brings this to bear on the particular issues of the client. But the therapist is not an instructor with knowledge of what a successful outcome should be, like rational thinking or skilled behaviour. Kelly (1969c) likened the therapeutic relationship to research supervision. Here, the therapist's expertise is restricted to the ways in which clients might carry their projects forward: what experiments to conduct and what conclusions to draw. But the responsibility of the direction of the project rests with clients, who know most about what they are aiming at and what they want. The outcome of therapy may well not be behavioural change, and what one wants at the beginning of the therapy process might not be the same as at the end. So it is very difficult to say in advance what an 'effective' end point would look like. Tom might seek therapy because he is often depressed as he gets older and thinks more about illness and death. He might imagine that a happier state of mind should ensue from successful therapy. But as Freud pointed out a century ago, common unhappiness is the lot of humankind. As we all get older, we frequently regret many things we did and opportunities we did not take. These events may be brought into sharp relief by a recognition of our mortality. What might be needed here is a coming to terms with life's inevitable pains and disappointments. What might be considered neurotic would be to engage in a systematic programme of denial; trying unsuccessfully to live the life of a man twenty years younger and competing in a race against time that cannot be won. Therapy here should not be about change, but about coming to terms with oneself and one's life.

At the start of this book, I made the point that psychological change and reconstruction was at the heart of the study of personality. I have argued that because we share human embodiment and a common culture, our commonality has been understated by much of psychology, but overstated by social constructionism. Although we have fashioned ourselves from the distal and proximal materials provided by society, we have also developed in ways that make each of us unique. In these late modern times, we reflect more on ourselves, think about how our lives could be better and see more opportunities to lead a more fulfilling existence. We live in a social climate that prizes individual fulfilment and we want to express ourselves as well as develop our particular strengths and potentials. The concepts and vocabulary of therapy have pervaded everyday language, and the science of personality and the prospect of personal change are inextricably mixed. The thesis of this book has been that this science of personality cannot be built on the causal explanations that are the hallmark of the natural sciences. Instead, it must be content with the understanding that characterises the human sciences of sociology, anthropology and history. Therapy does not consist of applying a set of personality spanners to tune behaviour to a high degree of efficiency. It is not necessarily about changing behaviour at all, although it is a necessary prerequisite to any change of this kind. It is about helping people to understand themselves in a way that gives them more options and degrees of freedom. But if understanding people is a practical necessity, it is also a moral imperative. Hinkle (1970) quotes Kelly as saying that his sociality corollary (the one that underlines the importance of construing the other's constructions) was in many ways at the centre of the psychology of personal constructs. He usually wrote about it in the context of the therapeutic relationship, where he emphasised that the therapist had to understand the client's construct system before there could be any psychological reconstruction. But he also felt that understanding others was something we *ought* to aim at. Pragmatists and existentialists alike have always rejected the ideal of a value-free psychology.

This issue has been elaborated by Rorty (1982), one of the current standard-bearers of pragmatism. He makes the point that we can never really separate a value-free description from an evaluation.

Even when I think 'that top's blue', I'm silently adding 'and I don't like it much!' And when we use the vocabulary of psychology – skilled, neurotic, introverted, for example – it is bound to carry some value or other. In fact, Rorty argues, the vocabulary of the social sciences wouldn't be much good if it weren't understandable to everybody else and if it couldn't be translated into policy that certainly should not be value-free. In a futile attempt to be value-free, social scientists have adopted the language of the natural sciences, adopting a distance from their subject material. Causal explanation is an example of this, a restricted type of understanding that aims at prediction and control. This will do the job nicely, he says, if we are trying to do something like evaluating artillery fire. But the aim of the social sciences is not like this; its job is to develop a vocabulary for moral reflection. The social sciences should interpret the actions of people who are marginal, problematic or puzzling:

> The reason why we invite the moronic psychopath to address the court before being sentenced is not in the hope for better explanations than expert psychiatric testimony has offered. We do so because he is, after all, one of us. By asking for his own account in his own words, we hope to decrease the chance of acting badly. What we hope for from social scientists is that they will act as interpreters for those with whom we are not sure how to talk. This is the same thing we hope for from our poets and dramatists and novelists. (Rorty, 1982: 202)

Now I think Rorty might have too much faith in 'expert psychiatric testimony', which is frequently couched in the language of objective thought. Nonetheless, he insists that the social sciences should be construed as on a continuum with artists who explore human existence with all its paradoxes and conflicts. There is also no special internal domain belonging to the psychologist, who is on a continuum with other social scientists. Ryle (1949) took the same position. When the term 'psychology' was coined, it was assumed that a Cartesian interior would be unlocked by it. Whereas people in everyday life, like novelists, detectives and salespeople, read others from their gestures, expressions and words, the psychologist was supposed to be able to get inside them and tell us what they were really up to. But when we exorcise Descartes' ghost, all psychologists are left with is the same evidence open to other non-psychologists. Ryle (1949) compared the professional geographer to a village postman in order to see what was scientific about geography. Whereas the postman knew his area better than any geographer, he did not use the geographer's dimensions and devise theories in the way the scientist would. In a similar way we ought to be able to compare, say, a novelist or a detective to a psychologist. They work with the same data as the psychologist, but: 'their handling of them would not be scientific. Theirs would correspond to a shepherd's weather-lore; his to a meterologist's science' (Ryle, 1949: 304). Understanding others is everybody's business, or ought to be. There is no doubt that some novelists, detectives and salespeople could teach the average psychologist a lot about reading others. Their knowledge is in no way inferior, but it is of a different order.

The psychology of personality is concerned with experience; with feelings, intentions and meaning. As Keen (1975) says, the benefit of an existential phenomenological approach is that it attempts to work with this material in a disciplined and systematic way. Its project is to clarify things and help us to think about ourselves in an honest and productive way. We look to the novelist to give us some idea about how other people think and feel. What we want from the personality theorist is something similar, but the psychologist's statements must be rooted more explicitly in evidence and theory. We all want to know what makes people tick – that's what attracted us to psychology in the first place. What we have to give up is the expectation that we will find answers deep inside; final explanations that will reveal everything and dispel all the mysteries and ambiguities of human action. But what we can hope for is better understanding that will enable us to live with both others and ourselves in a more generous, forgiving and constructive way.

References

Abercrombie, N. (1986) Knowledge, order and human autonomy, in J. Hunter and S. Ainley (eds) *Making Sense of Modern Times: Peter L. Berger and the Vision of Interpretive Sociology*, London: Routledge.

American Psychiatric Association (1994) *Diagnostic and Statistical Manual of Mental Disorders*, 4th edn (DSM-1V) Washington, DC: APA.

Anderson, R. (1992) *Clinical Papers on Klein and Bion*, London: Routledge.

APA website http://www.psych.org/public_info/ptsd.cfm, accessed 20 May 2003.

Archer, M. (2000) *Being Human: The Problem of Agency*, Cambridge: Cambridge University Press.

Argyle, M., Bryant. B. and Trower, P. (1974) Social skills training and psychotherapy, *Psychological Medicine*, **4**: 435–43.

Aronson, E., Wilson, T. and Akert, R. (2002) *Social Psychology*, 4th edn, Englewood Cliffs, NJ: Prentice Hall.

Ashworth, P. (2000) *Psychology and Human Nature*, Howe, East Sussex: Psychology Press.

Bakhurst, D. and Sypnowich, C. (1995) Problems of the social self, in D. Bakhurst and C. Sypnowich (eds) *The Social Self*, London: Sage.

Bandura, A. (1969) *Principles of Behaviour Modification*, New York: Holt, Rinehart & Winston.

Bandura, A. (1977) Self-efficacy: towards a unifying theory of behaviour change. *Psychological Review*, **84**: 191–215.

Bannister, D. (1980) The nonsense of effectiveness, *New Forum*, **13**.

Bannister, D. (1983) The internal politics of psychotherapy, in D. Pilgrim (ed.) *Psychology and Psychotherapy: Current Trends and Issues*, London: Routledge.

Baumeister, R. (1999) On the interface between personality and social psychology, in A. Pervin and O. John (eds) *Handbook of Personality: Theory and Research*, New York: Guilford.

Beck, A. (1976) *Cognitive Therapy and the Emotional Disorders*, Harmondsworth: Penguin.

Beck, A. (1991) Cognitive therapy: A thirty year retrospective. *American Psychologist*, **46**: 368–75.

Bem, D. (1972) Self-perception theory, in L. Berkowitz (ed.) *Advances in Experimental Social Psychology*, Vol. 6, New York: Academic Press.

Berger, P. (1963) *Invitation to Sociology*, Harmondsworth: Penguin.

Berger, P. and Luckmann, T. (1967) *The Social Construction of Reality*, Harmonds-worth: Penguin.

Berne, E. (1966) *Games People Play*, London: Andre Deutsch.

Billig, M. (1997) The dialogic unconscious: psychoanalysis, discursive psychol-ogy and the nature of repression, *British Journal of Social Psychology*, **36**(2): 139–60.

Blumer, H. (1969) *Symbolic Interactionism*, Englewood Cliffs, NJ: Prentice Hall.

Bordieu, P. (1998) *Practical Reason*, Cambridge: Polity.

Breuer, J. and Freud, S. (1956) Studies on hysteria, in J. Strachey (ed.) *Standard Edition of the Complete Works of Sigmund Freud* 2, London: Hogarth.

Burkitt, I. (1999) *Bodies of Thought: Embodiment, Identity and Modernity*, London: Sage.

Burr, V. (1995) *An Introduction to Social Constructionism*, London: Routledge.

Burr, V. and Butt, T. W. (1992) *Invitation to Personal Construct Psychology*, London: Whurr.

Butt, T. (1997) The existentialism of George Kelly, *Journal for the Society for Exis-tential Analysis*, **8**(1): 20–32.

Butt, T. (1998) Sociality, role, and embodiment, *Journal of Constructivist Psychol-ogy*, **11**(2): 105–16.

Butt, T. W. (2003) The phenomenological context of PCP, in F. Fransella (ed.) *International Handbook of Personal Construct Psychology*, Chichester: Wiley.

Butt, T. and Langridge, D. (2003) The construction of self: the public reach into the private sphere, *Sociology*, **37**(3): 477–94.

Butt, T., Burr, V. and Bell, R. (1997a) Fragmentation and the sense of self, *Con-structivism in the Human Sciences*, **2**: 12–29.

Butt, T., Burr, V. and Epting, F. (1997b) Core construing: Discovery or inven-tion?, in G. J. Neimeyer and R. A. Neimeyer (eds) *Advances in Personal Construct Theory*, Volume 4, New York: Springer.

Cattell, R. B. (1965) *The Scientific Analysis of Personality*, Harmondsworth: Penguin.

Chiari, G. and Nuzzo, M. L. (1996) Psychological constructivisms: a metatheo-retical differentiation, *Journal of Constructivist Psychology*, **9**: 163–84.

Cohen, S. and Taylor, L. (1976) *Escape Attempts: The Theory and Practice of Resis-tance to Everyday Life*, London: Allen Lane.

Costa, P. and McCrea, R. (1992) *NEO-PI-R: Professional manual*, Odessa, FL: Psychological Assessment Resources.

Craib, I. (1998) *Experiencing Identity*, London: Sage.

Craib, I. (2002) Psychotherapy: Social control and social criticism, *Psychotherapy Section Newsletter*, **32**: 13–17.

Crossley, N. (2001) *The Social Body: Habit, Identity and Desire*, London: Sage.

Davies, R. (ed.) (1994) *The Diaries of Kenneth Williams*, London: HarperCollins.

Day, W. (1977) On the behavioural analysis of self-deception and self-develop-ment, in T. Mischel (ed.) *The Self: Psychological and Philosophical Issues*, Oxford: Blackwell.

Dilthey, W. (1988) *Introduction to the Human sciences: An Attempt to Lay a Foundation for the Study of Society and History*, Detroit: Wayne State University Press.

Dryden, W. (1987) *Counselling Individuals: The Rational-Emotive Approach*, London: Whurr.

Elliott, A. (2001) *Concepts of the Self*, Cambridge: Polity.

Ellis, A. (1975) Rational-emotive therapy, in D. Bannister (ed.) *Issues and Approaches in the Psychological Therapies*, London: Wiley.

Ellis, A. (1987) On the origin and development of rational-emotive therapy, in W. Dryden (ed.) *Key Cases in Psychotherapy*, London: Croom Helm.

Erwin, E. (1978) *Behaviour Therapy: Scientific, Philosophical and Moral Foundations*, Cambridge: Cambridge University Press.

Eysenck, H. J. (1953) *Uses and Abuses of Psychology*, Harmondsworth: Penguin.

Eysenck, H. J. (1967) *The Biological Basis of Personality*, Springfield: Charles C. Thomas.

Eysenck, H. J. (1976) *Case Studies in Behaviour Therapy*, London: Routledge.

Eysenck, H. J. and Rackman, S. (1965) *The Causes and Cures of Neurosis*, San Diego: Knapp.

Fairbairn, W. R. D. (1952) *Psycho-Analyic Studies of the Personality*, London: Routledge

Farr, R. (1996) *The Roots of Modern Social Psychology*, Oxford: Blackwell.

Fingarette, H. (1969) *Self Deception*, London: Routledge.

Foucault, M. (1977) *Discipline and Punish: The Birth of the Prison*, London: Allen Lane.

Foucault, M. (1981) *The History of Sexuality*, Volume 1, Harmondsworth: Penguin.

Frankle, V. (1978) *The Unheard Cry for Meaning*, New York: Simon and Schuster.

Fransella, F. (ed.) (2003) *International Handbook of Personal Construct Psychology*, Chichester: Wiley.

Fransella, F. and Bannister, D. (1977) *A Manual for Repertory Grid Technique*, London: Academic Press.

Freud, S. (1953) The interpretation of dreams, in J. Strachey (ed.) *Standard Edition of the Complete Works of Sigmund Freud* 5, London: Hogarth Press.

Freud, S. (1957) The unconscious, in J. Strachey (ed.) *Standard Edition of the Complete Works of Sigmund Freud* 14, London: Hogarth Press.

Freud, S. (1962) The ego and the id, in J. Strachey (ed.) *Standard Edition of the Complete Works of Sigmund Freud* 19, London: Hogarth.

Gadamer, H. G. (1975) *Truth and Method*, Seabury: New York.

Gaugh, B. and McFadden, M. (2001) *Critical Social Psychology: An Introduction*, Basingstoke: Palgrave.

Gay, P. (1988) *Freud: A Life For Our Time*, London: Dent.

Gergen, K. (1985) The social constructionist movement in modern psychology, *American Psychologist*, **4**: 266–75.

Gergen, K. (1992) Towards a postmodern psychology, in S. Kvale (ed.) *Psychology and Postmodernism*, London: Sage.

Gergen, K. (1999) *An Invitation to Social Constructionism*, London: Sage.

Gergen, K. (2001) *Social Constructionism in Context*, London: Sage.

Giddens, A. (1984) *The Constitution of Society*, Cambridge: Polity.

Giddens, A. (1991) *Modernity and Self-Identity*, Cambridge: Polity.

Giddens, A. (1992) *The Transformation of Intimacy*, Cambridge: Polity.

Goffman, E. (1983) The interaction order, *American Sociological Review*, **48**(1): 1–17.

Goldberg, L. (1992) The development of markers for the Big Five factor structure. *Psychological Assessment*, **4**: 26–42.

Hammond, M., Howarth, J. and Keat, R. (1991) *Understanding Phenomenology*, Oxford: Blackwell.

Harré, R. (1976) *Personality*, Oxford: Blackwell.

Harré, R. (1986) An outline of the social constructionist viewpoint, in R. Harré (ed.) *The Social Construction of Emotions*, Oxford: Blackwell.

Harré, R. (1989) Language games and texts of identity, in J. Shotter and K. Gergen (eds) *Texts of Identity*, London: Sage.

Harré, R. and Gillett, G. (1994) *The Discursive Mind*, London: Sage.

Hebb, D. (1949) *The Organisation of Behaviour: A Neuropsychological Theory*, New York: Wiley.

Hinkle, D. (1970) The game of personal constructs, in D. Bannister (ed.) *Perspectives in Personal Construct Theory*, London: Academic Press.

Holland, R. (1970) George Kelly: constructive innocent and reluctant existentialist, in D. Bannister (ed.) *Perspectives in Personal Construct Theory*, London: Academic Press.

Holland, R. (1977) *Self in Social Context*, London: Macmillan.

Husserl, E. (1967) *Cartesian Meditations*, the Hague: Nijhoff.

Husserl, E. (1970) *The Crisis of European Sciences and Transcendental Phenomenology. An Introduction to Phenomenological Philosophy*, Evanston, IL: Northwestern University Press.

Ihde, D. (1986) *Experimental Phenomenology*, Albany: SUNY Press.

Joas, H. (1985) *G. H. Mead: A Contemporary Re-examination of His Thought*, Cambridge, MA: MIT Press.

Kanfer, F. and Phillips, J. (1970) *Learning Foundations of Behaviour Therapy*, New York: Wiley.

Kaufman, G. (1993) *The Psychology of Shame*, London: Routledge.

Keen, E. (1975) *A Primer in Phenomenological Psychology*, Washington, DC: Holt, Rinehart & Winston.

Kelly, G. A. (1955) *The Psychology of Personal Constructs*, New York: Norton.

Kelly, G. A. (1969a) Man's construction of his alternatives, in B. Maher (ed.) *Clinical Psychology and Personality: The Selected Papers of George Kelly*, London: Wiley.

Kelly, G.A. (1969b) Psychotherapy and the nature of man, in B. Maher (ed.) *Clinical Psychology and Personality: The Selected Papers of George Kelly*, London: Wiley.

Kelly, G. A, (1969c) The autobiography of a theory, in B. Maher (ed.) *Clinical Psychology and Personality: The Selected Papers of George Kelly*, London: Wiley.

Kelly, G. A. (1969d) Ontological acceleration, in B. Maher (ed.) *Clinical Psychology and Personality: The Selected Papers of George Kelly*, New York: Wiley.

Kelly, G. A. (1969e) The psychotherapeutic relationship, in B. Maher (ed.) *Clinical Psychology and Personality: The Selected Papers of George Kelly*, London: Wiley.

Kelly, G. A. (1969f) The language of hypothesis: man's psychological instrument, in B. Maher (ed.) *Clinical Psychology and Personality: The Selected Papers of George Kelly*, London: Wiley.

Klein, M. (1932) *The Psycho-Analysis of Children*, London: Hogarth.

Kovel, J. (1976) *A Complete Guide to Therapy*, Harmondsworth: Penguin.

Kvale, S. (1992) Postmodern psychology: a contradiction in terms?, in S. Kvale (ed.) *Psychology and Postmodernism*, London: Sage.

Langdridge, D. and Butt, T. W. (in press) The fundamental attribution error: a phenomenological critique, *British Journal of Social Psychology*.

Lazarus, A, (1987) When more is better, in W. Dryden (ed.) *Key Cases in Psychotherapy*, London: Croom Helm.

Macquarrie, J. (1972) *Existentialism: An Introduction, Guide and Assessment*, Harmonsworth: Penguin.

Maher, B. (ed.) (1969) *Clinical Psychology and Personality: The Selected Papers of George Kelly*, New York: Wiley.

Mair, J. M. M. (1977) The community of self, in D. Bannister (ed.) *New Perspectives in Personal Construct Theory*, London: Academic Press.

Malan, D. (1979) *Individual Psychotherapy and the Science of Psychodynamics*, London: Butterworth.

Markus, H. (1977) Self-schemata and processing information about the self, *Journal of Personality and Social Psychology*, **35**: 63–78.

Markus, H. and Nurius, P. (1986) Possible selves, *American Psychologist*, **41**: 954–69.

Mead, G. (1934) *Mind, Self and Society*, Chicago: University of Chicago Press.

Mead, G. (1982a) Social consciousness and the consciousness of meaning, in H. Thayer (ed.) *Pragmatism: The Classic Writings*, Indianapolis: Hackett.

Mead, G, (1982b) The social self, in H. Thayer (ed.) *Pragmatism: The Classic Writings*, Indianapolis: Hackett.

Meichenbaum, D. (1977) *Cognitive Behaviour Modification*, New York: Plenum.

Menand. L. (2002) *The Metaphysical Club*, London: HarperCollins.

Merleau-Ponty, M. (1962) *Phenomenology of Perception*, London: Routledge.

Merleau-Ponty, M. (1963) *The Structure of Behaviour*, Pittsburgh: Duquesne University Press.

Merleau-Ponty, M. (1964) The child's relations with others, in J. Edie (ed.) *The Primacy of Perception*, Nebraska: Northwestern University Press.

Merleau-Ponty, M. (1968) *The Visible and the Invisible*, Evanston: Northwestern University Press.

Merleau-Ponty, M. (1993) Phenomenology and psychoanalysis: Preface to *L'Oeuvre de Freud*, in K. Hoeller (ed.) *Merleau-Ponty and Psychology*, New Jersey: Humanities Press.

Meyer, V., Sharpe, R. and Chesser, E. (1976) Behavioural analysis and treatment of a complex case, in H. J. Eysenck (ed.) *Case Studies in Behaviour Therapy*, London: Routledge.

Milgram, S. (1963) Behavioural study of obedience. *Journal of Abnormal and Social Psychology*, **67**: 371–8.

Miller, A. (1985) *Thou Shalt Not Be Aware: Society's Betrayal of the Child*, London: Pluto Press.

Mischel, W. (1968) *Personality and Assessment*, London: Wiley.

Mischel, W. (1973) Towards a cognitive social learning reconceptualization of personality, *Psychological Review*, **80**: 252–83.

Mischel, W. (1993) *Introduction to Personality*, 5th edn, Fort Worth, TX: Harcourt Brace Jovanovich.

Mischel, W. and Mischel, H. (1977) Self-control and the self, in T. Mischel (ed.) *The Self: Psychological and Philosophical Issues*, Oxford: Blackwell.

Mischel, W. and Schoda, Y. (1995) A cognitive-affective system theory of personality: Reconceptualizing the invariances in personality and the role of situations, *Psychological Review*, **102**: 246–86.

Moran, D. (2000) *Introduction to Phenomenology*, London: Routledge.

Moran, D. and Mooney, T. (eds) (2002) *The Phenomenology Reader*, London: Routledge.

Moustakas, C. (1994) *Phenomenological Research Methods*, London: Sage.

Outhwaite, W. (1975) *Understanding Social Life: The Method Called Verstehen*, London: Allen & Unwin.

Pervin, L. and John, O. (2001) *Personality: Theory and Research*, 8th edn, Chichester: Wiley.

Plummer, K. (1995) *Telling Sexual Stories: Power, Change and Social Worlds*, London: Routledge.

Potter, J. and Wetherell, M. (1987) *Discourse and Social Psychology: Beyond Attitudes and Behaviour*, London: Sage.

Potter, J. and Wetherell, M. (1995) Discourse analysis, in J. Smith, R. Harré and L. Van Langenhove (eds) *Rethinking Methods in Psychology*, London: Sage.

Rackman, S. (1980) *Fear and Courage*, London: Freeman.

Rickman, H. P. (1997) Dilthey's hermeneutics, *Journal of the Society for Existential Anlysis*, **8**(2): 46–55.

Ricoeur, P. (1970) *Freud and Philosophy: An Essay on Interpretation*, New Haven: Yale University Press.

Robins, R., Gosling, S. and Craik, K. (1999) An empirical analysis of trends in psychology, *American Psychologist*, **54**: 117–28.

Rogers, C. (1951) *Client-Centered Therapy*, Boston: Houghton Mifflin.

Rogers, C. (1980) *A Way of Being*, Boston: Houghton Mifflin.

Rorty, R. (1982) Method, social science and social hope, in R. Rorty (ed.) *Consequences of Pragmatism*, New York: Harvester Wheatsheaf.

Rosenthal, S. and Bourgeois, P. (1991) *Mead and Merleau-Ponty: Toward a Common Vision*, Albany: State University Press of New York.

Ross, L. and Nisbett, R. (1991) *The Person and the Situation: Perspectives of Social Psychology*, New York: McGraw-Hill.

Rowan, J. (1990) *Subpersonalities: The People Inside Us*, London: Routledge.

Ryle, G. (1949) *The Concept of Mind*, London: Hutchinson.

Sartre, J.-P. (1948) *Existentialism and Humanism*, London: Methuen.

Sartre, J.-P. (1958) *Being and Nothingness*, London: Methuen.

Schacter, S. and Singer, J. (1962) Cognitive, social and physiological determinants of emotional states, *Psychological Review*, **69**: 379–99.

Scheff, T. (1966) *Being Mentally Ill: A Sociological Theory*, Chicago: Aldine.

Sewell, K. (1997) Posttraumatic stress: Towards a constructivist model of psychotherapy, in G. Neimeyer and R. Neimeyer (eds) *Advances in Personal Construct Psychology*, Volume 4, Greenwich, CT: JAI Press.

Shotter, J. (1993) *Cultural Politics of Everyday Life*, Buckingham: Open University Press.

Shotter, J. (1995) Dialogical psychology, in J. Smith, R. Harré and L. Van Langenhove (eds) *Rethinking Psychology*, London: Sage.

Skinner, B. F. (1974) *About Behaviourism*, New York: Random House.

Smail, D. (1993) *The Origins of Unhappiness: A New Understanding of Personal Distress*, London: HarperCollins.

Smith, M. and Glass, G. (1977) Meta-analysis of psychotherapy outcome studies, *American Psychologist*, **32**: 752–60.

Smith, J., Harré, R. and Van Langenhove, L. (1995) *Rethinking Methods in Psychology*, London: Sage.

Snow, D. and Anderson, L. (2002) Salvaging the self, in A. Branaman (ed.) *Self and Society*, Oxford: Blackwell.

Spinelli, E. (1989) *The Interpreted World: An Introduction to Phenomenological Psychology*, London: Sage.

Spinelli, E. (1994) *Demystifying Therapy*, London: Constable.

Spinelli, E. (1995) The unconscious: an idea whose time has gone? in H. Cohn and S. du Plock (eds) *Existential Challenges to Psychotherapeutic Theory and Practice*, London: Society for Existential Analysis.

Stearns, C. and Stearns, P (1988) *Emotion and Social Change*, New York: Holmes & Meier.

Stoller, R. (1986) *Sexual Excitement: The Dynamics of Erotic Life*, London: Karnac Books.

Symington, N. (1986) *The Analytic Experience: Lectures from the Tavistock*, London: Routledge.

Szasz, T. (1970) *Ideology and Insanity*, New York: Anchor Books.

Thayer, H. (1982) *Pragmatism: The Classic Writings*, Indianapolis: Hackett.

Toates, F. (2001) *Biological Psychology: an Integrative Approach*, Harlow: Prentice Hall.

Toulmin, S. (1961) *Foresight and Understanding*, London: Hutchinson.

Van Boven, L., Kamada, A. and Gilovich, T. (1999) The perceiver as perceived: Everyday intuitions about the correspondence bias. *Journal of Personality and Social Psychology*, **77**: 1188–99.

van Deurzen, E. (2002) *Existential Counselling and Psychotherapy in Practice*, 2nd edn, London: Sage.

van Deurzen-Smith, E. (1995) Questioning the power of psychotherapy: Is Jeffrey Masson onto something? in H. Cohn and S. du Plock (eds) *Existential Challenges to Psychotherapeutic Theory and Practice*, London: Society for Existential Analysis.

van Deurzen-Smith, E. (1997) *Everyday Mysteries: Existential Dimensions of Psychotherapy*, London: Routledge.

Walsh, D. (1998) Structure/agency, in C. Jenks (ed.) *Core Sociological Dichotomies*, London: Sage.

Warnke, G. (1987) *Gadamer: Hermeneutics, Tradition and Reason*, Cambridge: Polity.

Warren, W. (1992) Subjecting and objecting in personal construct psychology, in A. Thomson and P. Cummins (eds) *European Perspectives in Personal Construct Psychology*, Lincoln: European Personal Construct Association.

Westen, D. (1998) The scientific legacy of Sigmund Freud: Toward a psychodynamically informed psychological science, *Psychological Bulletin*, **124**(3): 333–71.

Willig, C. (1999) *Applied Discourse Analysis: Social and Psychological Interventions*, Buckingham: Open University Press.

Winnicott, D. W. (1971) *Playing and Reality*, London: Tavistock.

Wittgenstein, L. (1972) *Philosophical Investigations*, Oxford: Blackwell.

Zajonc, R. (1980) Feeling and thinking preferences need no inferences, *American Psychologist*, **35**: 151–75.

Author Index

Subject Index

189